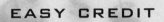
EASY CREDIT

EASY CREDIT

ANN E. WEISS

TWENTY-FIRST CENTURY BOOKS
Brookfield, Connecticut

01-457

Library of Congress Cataloging-in-Publication Data
Weiss, Anne.
Easy credit / Anne Weiss.
p. cm.
Includes bibliographical references and index.
Summary: Presents a history of credit from ancient times to
today's worldwide use of credit cards, detailing the advantages,
disadvantages, and effects of credit.
ISBN 0-7613-1503-9 (lib. bdg.)
1. Credit cards. [1. Credit. 2. Credit cards.] I. Title.
HG3755.7.W45   2000
332.7'43—dc21   99-462150

Published by Twenty-First Century Books
A Division of The Millbrook Press, Inc.
2 Old New Milford Road
Brookfield, Connecticut 06804
www.millbrookpress.com

This book is dedicated to those friends and family members who shared their credit stories with me. "Sally," the young Brooklyn woman, the man who reads The Nation, *and all the rest—you know who you are, and I thank you.*

CONTENTS

ONE
CHARGE IT!

Jennifer Dahlin was thrilled when the credit-card application turned up in her mailbox. To the sixteen-year-old California girl, a plastic credit card seemed just the ticket to whisk her magically away from her cramped, penny-pinching existence and into a wonderful new world of style and luxury.

Up until then, Jennifer had known little but poverty. When she was younger, she and her family sometimes found themselves without a roof over their heads. Hunger was an everyday reality. "We used to play this game about what we'd eat if we had food," Jennifer says now.

Jennifer was twelve when she landed her first job, selling door-to-door. In her early teens, she worked at video stores, pet shops, and fast-food places. By the age of fifteen she had moved into an apartment with friends and was supporting herself—barely—by scooping ice cream at a Baskin-Robbins. Then came the credit-card offer.

A credit card of her own! A small plastic rectangle, little more than 3 inches (7.6 centimeters) long and a couple of inches (5 centimeters) high, with an account number and the name "Jennifer Dahlin" embossed on the front. A card that she could present at practically any boutique, fast-food restaurant, music store, or other place of business. A card that could be run through a machine that would "read" the information it contained about Jennifer's account. A card that would keep track of every item Jennifer charged, note when and where she had charged it, and how much it cost. A card that would enable her to walk away with anything she wanted—clothes, makeup, pizza, jewelry, tapes—anything!

What was more, the card would, according to the application, carry a $2,000 line of credit. "Credit" refers to a system of doing business by trusting that a person will pay at a later date for goods or services provided. A $2,000 line of credit meant Jennifer would be able to "spend" up to that amount instantly without touching a cent of her own meager income. Jennifer could hardly believe her good fortune.

It was only when she studied the application more closely that Jennifer realized it was not actually addressed to her. The application, and the envelope it had come in, bore another woman's name. No matter. "I figured if I sent it back naming me as a secondary cardholder I could get my own card," Jennifer explains.

Jennifer also overlooked the fact that since she was not yet eighteen years old, she was too young to apply for a credit card on her own. People under age eighteen will receive a card only if an adult also signs the application. The adult cosigner promises to make good on any bills the young cardholder does not—or cannot—pay. Jennifer knew nothing of all that. She signed the application and dropped it in the mail. Within days, a shiny new Discover card was tucked into her wallet.

Jennifer was nothing if not generous with the card. "The very first thing I charged was a gift for my boyfriend." She took her roommates to nice restaurants. "It felt so good being able to slap my credit card down on the table." Christmas was coming, so Jennifer went shopping. "I gave my boyfriend everything he wanted—video games, new shoes, two suits, and lots of toys." There were goodies for Jennifer's girlfriends, as well. "The best feeling I had was Christmas morning when my friends saw all their presents."

Jennifer's elation did not survive long into the new year. The Discover card bill that arrived in January came close to $2,000.

Not that Jennifer had to pay the full amount all at once. Companies like the one that issued her card require cardholders to make only a relatively small minimum payment each month. The rest of the money due—the balance—remains to be paid later. Some credit-card users take months, even years, to pay off balances of just a few thousand dollars.

As we will see in more detail in Chapter Four, credit-card issuers charge cardholders for the privilege of postponing payment in this way. That charge, called interest, is calculated as a percentage of the total amount owed. A cardholder who is being charged 10 percent interest, for example, may have to pay back $1,100 for every $1,000 borrowed ($1,000 plus one tenth of $1,000, or $100 in interest). In addition to interest, credit-card issuers may tack on service fees for certain transactions such as withdrawing money from an Automated Teller Machine (ATM). An issuer may also impose monetary penalties when payments do not come in until after their due date.

Jennifer managed to make the minimum Discover card payment for January. But a few days later when she tried to use the card to get a cash advance from an ATM, the money was denied. She telephoned Discover to complain—and was shocked to learn that the card she was using was listed as having been stolen. Jennifer hadn't stolen the card, of course, but she *had* put her own name on a credit-card application intended for another person. That meant, as Discover officials made plain, that Jennifer could be charged with the crime of credit-card fraud. "They said, 'Pay the $1,600 balance or we'll turn your case over to the police,'" she recalls.

CREDIT CRUNCHES

Coming up with anything like $1,600 in cash was out of the question for Jennifer. The authorities were called in. Jennifer was arrested, taken to the police station, photographed, and fingerprinted. To give her an idea of what her life would be like if she was convicted of fraud, a detective showed the terrified girl through the women's jail.

In the end Jennifer was lucky. The judge who heard her case understood that she had not realized that what she was doing was wrong, and that she regretted having done it. Jennifer was not sentenced to prison. Instead the judge ordered her to repay the entire debt within six months and to perform forty hours of community service.[1] In a situation like Jennifer's, such service might consist of talking to middle- or high-school students about how credit cards work and what constitutes credit-card fraud.

Without really meaning to, Jennifer Dahlin had committed a credit-card crime that nearly got her into very serious trouble indeed. But she had made another mistake as well. Jennifer had gone credit-card crazy. She had "maxed out" on her card, borrowing the maximum amount—$2,000—of the credit she (or rather, someone else) had been offered. And she borrowed that money when there was no possibility at all that she could pay it back.

Plenty of other people make similar mistakes. Many who do so end up in a deeper financial hole than Jennifer did. Consider Hal McCabe.

At age eighteen, Hal had good reason to want to borrow money. He was set on a college education, and his mother—divorced and working at two jobs to make ends meet—was unable to offer much help. So Hal took out a loan for his tuition money. That's a reasonable and commonplace thing to do. With college costing thousands of dollars a year, very few young men and women can afford to attend without student loans.

But besides borrowing for college, Hal acquired a number of credit cards. He used them for daily expenses: food, transportation, books. He also used them to supply himself with luxuries: new clothes, fancy dates, entertainment. He borrowed $2,500 for a down payment on a used car and took out an auto loan to make the monthly payments. Nearly half a year after graduating from college, Hal was over $80,000 in debt—and not yet earning a salary.

Luckily for him, Hal found a $28,000-a-year job as a producer for America Online, the Internet server. It took time, but he managed to pay off his entire debt. What did he do then? Immediately started running up new credit-card bills. Within months, Hal was indebted again to the tune of $32,000. On top of that he was planning to buy his mother a new car.

Why was Hal so willing to sink back into debt? He wanted the good things in life and he wanted them right away, without having to wait and save up for them. "You can't max out your life if you don't max out your card sometimes," he says.[2]

Many Americans would agree with that philosophy. Not Amy Maxwell, though. Amy learned the hard way that maxing out on credit can mean not an enhanced lifestyle, but a more restricted one.

During her freshman year at American University in Washington, D.C., Amy applied for and got three Visa cards. One had a credit limit of $2,000. Another allowed her to spend $5,000. The third let her go up to $10,000.

Amy loved her cards. She used them for compact discs and videos, clothes, and restaurant meals. By the end of the year she was $17,000 in debt. No longer able to afford the tuition bills at expensive American University, Amy moved back to her parents' home in upstate New York and enrolled at a nearby community college. She found a full-time job and began trying to erase her history of debt.

Erasing it is essential for Amy—otherwise she will be stuck with a bad credit record. That record could make it tough, if not impossible, for her to borrow money in the future. Yet borrow she must. How can she buy a car without an auto loan? How can she hope to own a house without a home mortgage loan from a bank? Amy is determined to repair her credit history. She also wants to make it harder for others to get into the kind of financial mess she did. In her spare time, Amy campaigns for state laws that would keep credit-card issuers from tempting young people with the kind of credit-card offers that led her so deeply into debt.[3]

It's hard to predict how long it will be before Amy Maxwell is in the clear again financially. As Mark Nyman and Elizabeth Genel of Milford, Connecticut, could tell her, it may take years.

Nyman and Genel are married. Both went to college and graduated from law school. Although they are in their thirties, the two still owe $172,000 in education loans. The interest rate on those loans is 8 percent a year. Nyman practices law and earns good pay, but Genel does not use her law degree. She borrowed $100,000 (at 10 percent interest) to open a luxury cosmetics business. So far, the business is not bringing in enough money for her to take home any salary. The couple bought a condominium apartment with a $135,000 mortgage. They borrowed $30,000 from relatives, and pay $237 a month on their car. Outstanding (unpaid) credit-card debt amounts to another $25,000. In total, nearly three quarters of the money Nyman and Genel spend each month goes toward paying off their combined debts. They worry that they will never be able to afford children or enjoy retirement later in life.[4]

BANKRUPTCY AND BEYOND

Unpaid debt can have other serious consequences. Drew Hart is twenty-six and lives in Washington, D.C. He had fourteen separate credit accounts while he was in college, and graduated owing $20,000. Hart's solution to his financial dilemma: filing for bankruptcy.

Under U.S. law, individuals can go to court to declare themselves bankrupt—unable to pay their debts. Generally the court excuses virtually all of the debt. Creditors—companies that issue credit cards, banks, and other types of lenders—assume the loss as one of the risks of doing business. In 1997 a record 1.3 million Americans filed for bankruptcy.[5]

Drew Hart did not complete his bankruptcy filing, but he did join the U.S. military and accept an overseas assignment. Legally, his creditors could not pursue him once he was outside the United States. Out of the military and back at home, Hart promptly started adding new credit-card debts to his old ones. "I have no problem putting off my bills," he told a reporter for *The Wall Street Journal*.

His creditors, however, do have a problem. And they have ways of seeing to it that Hart does, too. According to Dwayne Heisler, who works as a debt collector for various creditors, people like Hart don't understand how much trouble they can be in.

Just as Hart himself went to court to escape his creditors, so his creditors can go to court to try to get their money back. If that happens a judge may order Hart's employer to "garnishee" his wages. That will mean that a certain amount of money will be taken out of Hart's paycheck each week. The garnisheed money will go directly to his creditors. Or the judge might authorize law enforcement officers to seize some of Hart's property—a car or a stereo system perhaps. That property will be sold and the money handed over to its rightful owners. Heisler says that some debtors seem to think that their problem is just going to disappear. "It's not," he warns.[6]

THE SMART USE OF CREDIT

Just because people like Drew Hart, Amy Maxwell, and others have gotten into credit trouble doesn't mean that all debt is bad. For millions of people, debt is a tool that can help them achieve a better, more satisfying way of life than they otherwise could.

We've already seen hints of this. There would be few college graduates without education loans. Doctors, social workers, men and women with business degrees, and other professionals would be in short supply. So would vocational school graduates such as plumbers, truck drivers, electricians, landscapers, and carpenters. Without home mortgage and auto loans, how many people could own a house or a car? Personal transportation, a home, an education that enables a person to earn a living—most of us would consider these necessities, not luxuries. Without debt many of these things would be out of reach for the majority of middle-class working people.

Debt can also bring luxuries within reach of ordinary people. In some instances it may be smart to take advantage of that fact. College, for example, can cost anywhere from a few thousand dollars a year at a state-funded university to over $30,000 a year at a top private school. A Harvard College graduate may wind up with a bigger debt than someone with a degree from Mid-State U., but she will also have had a different educational experience and perhaps a greater earning potential. A teenager who needs to drive to an after-school job may have to choose between paying outright for a car that's close to breaking down and borrowing— perhaps from his parents—for one in better condition. Does he want to avoid debt at all costs? Or is it more important for him to have a car he can depend upon to get him to work so he can keep on earning?

Credit may even be used for a one-time splurge like a special family vacation, a wedding, or a trip to see a relative in a distant part of the country. Splurgers, however, should be sure they will be able to repay the loan quickly. If they miss payments, they risk facing high interest charges and penalties.

Credit is also good to have in time of emergency. ATM cards allow users to pocket cash—for food, gas, roadside car repair, or other essentials—at thousands of locations twenty-four hours a day. Telephone cards, both the kind that let a person charge calls and the prepaid variety, often come in handy. A person might use a credit card to pay a hospital bill that health insurance doesn't cover. Credit cards are also useful for reserving tickets and hotel rooms over the phone. Employees at car rental agencies require proof of good credit, in the form of a major credit card, before they will let anyone drive off in one of their vehicles. Credit cards are especially convenient for people who need to keep track of their purchases, such as those who travel on business and whose expenses will be paid by an employer.

Few Americans have to be convinced of the usefulness of credit. More than people of any other nationality, Americans have adopted a "Charge it!" way of thinking. According to U.S. government figures, overall consumer debt, including mortgages and car loans as well as credit-card debt and every other sort of borrowing, hit $1.28 trillion before the end of 1998.[7] A few months earlier, Americans had owed over $422 billion on their credit cards alone—double their 1993 credit-card debt.[8] People in four fifths of all U.S. homes possess at least one credit card.[9] Most have several. It's a similar story in Canada, where many people also carry debit cards.[10] Like credit cards, debit cards are used to make purchases and take money from ATMs. With debit cards, though, the money spent or withdrawn is taken out of funds already on deposit in a cardholder's bank account. No borrowing is involved.

The modern credit industry is huge—and growing. Its growth seems remarkable, all the more so given how new much of the industry really is.

It was not until well into the twentieth century that bank loans for the purpose of buying big-ticket items such as automobiles became popular. The credit card as we know it first appeared less than fifty years ago. As recently as the 1980s, over half the nation's major stores and other retail outlets refused to honor Visa or MasterCard.[11] Today's consumers use credit cards to charge everything from groceries and postage stamps to world cruises, charitable donations, and their income tax. Within the next few years, some financial experts predict, computers and the Internet will once again transform the credit industry.

Yet credit itself is not new. It is old, older than computers, older than credit cards, older than auto loans, older even than money. Hundreds of years before the first coins were minted, thousands of years before paper money was invented, men and women were borrowing and lending, going into debt and charging interest.

Credit is as ancient as civilization.

TWO
CREDIT FROM ANCIENT TIMES

Human beings have always had mixed feelings about credit. From the beginning they have accepted the fact that people are sometimes going to have to borrow. A hungry family may be forced to go into debt to pay for food. A farmer may need to borrow seed—or borrow the means of buying it—in order to plant a crop.

People further know that lenders provide a valuable service. What is more, they understand that lenders provide that service at some cost to themselves. What if a borrower cannot repay a loan? Then the lender has lost money or other property, property that may have taken hard work and considerable time to earn and accumulate. Even if a loan is repaid, the lender has lost the use of the property loaned during the time it was in someone else's hands. It is in order to make up for the risks and disadvantages of extending credit that lenders charge interest.

No wonder we feel confused about credit. On the one hand, it does seem fair for lenders to earn compensation for the service they offer. On the other, is it right to make desperate people pay for the privilege of borrowing when they have no other choice? Is it moral for the rich to wring profits from the misfortunes of the poor?

Religion teaches us that it is not. In the words of the Koran, the holy book of Islam, "God has permitted trading and made usury unlawful."[1] The dictionary defines usury as "an excessively high rate of interest." The Bible of the Christian and Jewish faiths similarly forbids usury. "Take thee no usury," says the Old Testament book of Leviticus.

Moreover, the Bible and the Koran characterize usury not only as excessive interest but as any interest whatsoever. "Thou shalt not give him thy money upon usury," Leviticus goes on, "nor lend him thy victuals [food] for increase." In other words, lenders should extend credit interest-free. They should earn no profit at all. Another Old Testament book, Ezekiel, repeats the ban on lending for interest: "He that…hath taken increase: shall he then live? he shall not live:…he shall surely die."[2] The Koran urges those who have lent to people in financial trouble to forgive the debt. "If you waive the sum as alms [regard the loan as charity] it will be better for you."[3]

So that's the dilemma. The religious ideal condemns the charging of interest. The practical workaday world demands it. Can the two be reconciled?

CREDIT IN MESOPOTAMIA

The question predates the Bible and the Koran. Long before either was written, kings in the ancient world were trying to strike a balance between the rights and obligations of borrowers and lenders. The first recorded official interest rates were set nearly four thousand years ago in the land called Mesopotamia. Mesopotamia lay between the Tigris and Euphrates rivers in what is now Iraq. Its name comes from the Greek words, *mesos*, "middle," and *potamos*, "river."

In about 1950 B.C., the king of the city of Eshnunna, on the east bank of the Tigris, put a limit on the amount of interest a lender could collect. That limit was 20 percent of the sum loaned.

The king also made it easier for borrowers to honor their debts by letting them pay in grain for loans made in silver. His decrees were part of the code of justice under which he ruled Eshnunna. Ancient codes like Eshnunna's were scratched onto clay tablets or carved into stone monuments and temple walls where they commanded respect, even from those who could not read.

Another Mesopotamian reference to borrowing and interest comes from the city of Sippur. There, a man named Puzurum, son of Ili-kadari, borrowed a certain weight of silver from the supply kept at the temple of the god Shamash. "At the time of harvest," an ancient document notes, "he will repay the silver and the interest on it."

A third mention of credit is contained in the Code of Hammurabi, the most widely known code of the very ancient world. This code was proclaimed about two hundred years after the Eshnunna code was drawn up.

Hammurabi was king of Babylon, southwest of Eshnunna. He conquered cities throughout Mesopotamia and ruled them from about 1763 B.C. until his death approximately thirteen years later. Hammurabi, too, limited interest to 20 percent of the amount lent and allowed borrowers to repay in grain if they had no silver.[4] According to his code, a man could sell his wife, son, or daughter into slavery if need be to settle a debt. Yet the king took care to offer a measure of protection to those sold. "...[F]or three years, they shall work in the house of their purchaser or master; in the fourth year they shall be given their freedom."[5] To let the lender keep them enslaved for more than three years, Hammurabi evidently thought, smacked of what we would call usury.

Slaves could be used to repay debts in Mesopotamia because they, like grain and silver, were considered a medium of exchange, a form of money. All three fall into the category of "commodity money."

COMMODITY MONEY

Commodity money, unlike the paper money and coins we use today, is useful in and of itself. Slaves provide labor. Grain can be eaten. Silver and other metals can be fashioned into weapons, tools, or ornaments. Paper money and coins made of cheap metals like copper and nickel are not particularly useful in any of those ways. They are simply a means of exchange.

Commodity money has been used throughout human history. Gold is an almost universally popular type of commodity money. Other examples include salt, silk, and spices; almonds, once used in parts of India; and the corn, beads, furs, and other goods exchanged among the peoples of what were to become the Americas. Butter and dried codfish once served as commodity money in Norway.

Commodity money remains in use in the modern world, especially in troubled times. After World War II ended in Europe in 1945, millions of victims of the conflict resorted to cigarettes, chocolate, and chewing gum—gifts from U.S. soldiers—in place of the money they did not have.[6] In the late 1990s hunting licenses were substituting for money in financially troubled Russia. Russian coins and bills were worth so little at that time that some public employees were delighted when the government offered to "pay" them with elk-hunting permits instead of cash. The opportunity to hunt for food was more valuable to them than money.

Yet widespread as the use of commodity money has always been, such money has its disadvantages. It tends to be bulky and cumbersome to move around. As food, it can spoil. Slaves may escape or die from disease or abuse. Even gold and silver bullion—gold and silver in bulk, rather than in the form of coins—can be awkward to use as money.

In ancient Mesopotamia, for example, bullion was shaped into bricklike ingots. It also existed in the form of smaller, odd-sized pieces and as thin, wiry strands. The worth of each bit of bullion could be determined only by weighing it on a scale or balance. Anyone doing business had to own a scale and be expert in its use. He or she had to be able to judge the purity and value of every ingot, scrap, and strand that might come along.[7] Buying and selling was therefore a complex, lengthy business. It was a big business, too—literally. A single ingot of precious metal might purchase an entire warehouse full of grain or cloth. Small-scale transactions were not yet the rule.

So it was that commerce in the most ancient times was a matter for the rich, trained, and educated few. Trading, borrowing, and lending were outside the experience of the great majority. At most, ordinary people engaged in barter, informally exchanging limited supplies of goods and services. A man might trade a day's work for food and shelter, for instance. A woman might swap eggs for milk. There was no money as we know it.

Then, in the seventh century B.C. someone invented coins. According to Jack Weatherford, a writer, anthropologist, and college professor who has studied ancient civilizations worldwide, those coins transformed the way human beings lived and thought. They made it possible for almost anyone to participate in commercial activity, adding new urgency to old questions about the morality of lending and the charging of interest.

COINS AND THE MARKETPLACE

The first coins appeared in Lydia, a small kingdom between the Black Sea and the Mediterranean Sea, around 630 B.C. The coins were oval, an inch (2.5 centimeters) or so long and 0.5 inch (1.2 centimeters) thick. Each was minted—stamped—with the image of a lion's head. The image assured users that the coins were genuine, issued by order of the king. Even people who couldn't use a scale or had no idea of the value of precious metals could recognize a Lydian coin. They knew at a glance what each one was worth and how much it would buy.

Lydia's coins were an immediate success. As the minting process became more sophisticated, coins assumed the round, flat shape we know today. Within a short time rulers all around the Mediterranean were minting coins of their own.

Coins revolutionized commercial life. Trade was no longer only for wealthy merchants who bought and sold in bulk. Now, a coin or two purchased a few days' worth of food or just enough cloth for a single family. Coins also bought labor and people began being paid in cash, rather than bartering work for food or shelter. The new system was convenient and flexible. Workers could use the coins they earned in any way they wanted, spending their wages on whatever suited them. For the first time, ordinary folk had buying power.

That power helped to create retail markets. In the marketplace, merchants gathered to sell a wide variety of goods, from staples—grain, oil, pottery, and the like—to jewelry, musical instruments, rich textiles, and other luxury items. All could be sold in small quantities directly to individual consumers. The first retail markets were established in Lydia, but by the sixth century B.C., the city-states of what is now Greece boasted the world's busiest trading centers.

It was in the Greek marketplace, the agora, Weatherford says, that modern Western civilization got its start. As people grew accustomed to dealing with money, exchanging coins for food or a day's work, they became used to counting and working with numbers. Mathematics was born. From math, science and other branches of learning developed. By the fourth century B.C., the Greek soldier, politician, and writer Xenophon had introduced the idea of *oikonomikos*—"economics." As the word was originally used, it meant "skilled in managing a household or estate."[8] Today we define economics as the science concerned with the production and consumption of goods and services.

Besides being a place where merchants and consumers could meet and do business, the agora allowed for the buying and selling of money itself. In the Greek city of Athens, money changers set up shop alongside merchants, offering to exchange Athenian coins for the foreign coins of traders from other Mediterranean cities. The money changers charged a fee for this service. They also accepted deposits from foreign visitors who needed a safe place to keep their money and other valuables while they were traveling. On occasion, money changers agreed to lend some of this money—at 12 percent interest—to citizens in need of cash. Athenians could also borrow from the store of bullion kept at the temple of the city's leading goddess, Athena.[9]

Athenians, like earlier peoples, were of two minds about credit. It might be convenient to be able to borrow from Athena or a money changer, but was it right? Philosophers like Plato (427?–347 B.C.) and Aristotle (384–322 B.C.) condemned the practice.[10] As Plato saw it, dishonesty always pays better than honesty. Therefore, he reasoned, people who become wealthy— money changers, for example—must necessarily have acted dishonestly. Aristotle, for his part, came up with a way of getting around any need for credit. Why not allow poor people to pay less than rich ones for the goods they buy? he suggested. With prices adjusted to individual income, no one would be forced to borrow.[11] It's probably safe to assume that the traders and money changers of Aristotle's day didn't think much of that idea!

In ancient Rome, too, writers and thinkers pondered the morality of lending and charging interest. Rome, located in what is now Italy, was founded about seven and a half centuries B.C. From then until shortly before the birth of Jesus Christ, the city was governed as a republic. In 31 B.C. it came under the control of the first of a long series of emperors. Rome, and the vast area its armies had conquered throughout Europe and the Near East, would be subject to imperial rule for another five hundred years.

For centuries Rome was a wealthy city. Much of its wealth circulated in the form of silver coins, denarii in Latin, the language of the place. Starting in 269 B.C., denarii (singular, denarius) were minted at the temple of the goddess Juno Moneta—Juno, protector of Rome. From the goddess's name come our words "money" and "mint." Another English word for money, "currency," also traces its origins to Juno's temple. So rapidly did silver denarii pour forth from the mint that Romans compared them to a fast-flowing stream. *Currere* is Latin for "to flow" or "to run."[12] Even our word "credit" comes from the Latin *credo*, "I trust." As we saw in Chapter One, the idea of credit is based upon trust.

For all their wealth, Romans were great consumers of credit. During the city's last years as a republic, politicians regularly took out loans to buy their way into public office. Loans were also used to finance wars. Julius Caesar (100–44 B.C.), whose military victories added so much to what was to become the Roman Empire, borrowed heavily to pay for his campaigns. At one point Caesar owed 25 million denarii. To get an idea of the size of that debt, consider that a soldier in Caesar's army could expect to earn just 225 denarii a year.[13]

Not everyone in Rome approved of all the borrowing. Some denounced any lending for interest. But others argued that not all loans are the same, and that some serve a useful purpose. They pointed to what they saw as a difference between "productive credit" and "consumptive credit."

Productive credit was money borrowed with the idea of investment—money to be used to buy farmland or set up in trade. Consumptive credit involved borrowing money and squandering it on consumer goods that are soon gone. Such credit was wasteful. Productive credit, by contrast, was beneficial because increasing the availability of food and other goods helps everyone. In time, Roman law came to reflect this distinction. Productive credit was permitted and interest limits set.[14]

Rich as Rome was, its wealth eventually ran out. Emperors spent lavishly on temples, homes, and country estates. They waged one expensive war after another. When the bills came due, they often found themselves without enough silver denarii to pay them. The emperors' way of dealing with that problem was to order old coins melted down and new ones minted.

Actually there was more to it than that. The emperors' precise orders were to melt the old coins, mix the silver with a base, non-precious metal, and use the mixture to mint new coins. Every cycle of melting and reminting put more coins into circulation. With so many coins on hand, Romans still had plenty to spend. However, since each new denarius contained less silver than each older one, each was less valuable than before. In fact, Romans were growing poorer, not richer. Back in the first century A.D. their coins had been nearly 100 percent silver. Two hundred years later they were almost 100 percent nonsilver.[15] So worthless had coins become that most people in the western part of the Roman Empire simply stopped using them. Only east of the Italian peninsula did coins continue to circulate widely.

Rome's wealth was gone. So, after 476, was Rome itself, invaded and destroyed by barbarian tribes from the north and east. The so-called Dark Ages had fallen across western Europe.

CRUSADERS
AND
CREDITORS

The Dark Ages lasted for five hundred years. During those centuries the majority of Europeans lived as peasants, working their lives away for the great lord or landowner on whose estate they happened to have been born. There was little buying or selling. Some kings and chieftains did mint coins, but even among the rich their exchange was rare.[16] Commodity money and bartering made comebacks.

Not until the Crusades began late in the eleventh century did commerce pick up again in Europe.

The Crusades were military campaigns undertaken by European Christians determined to take back the Holy Land, where Jesus had been born and died. The Holy Land lay east of the Mediterranean. Over the years it had come under the control of Muslims, followers of Islam. Now, Muslim rulers were keeping Christian pilgrims from visiting the sacred sites where Jesus had preached the gospel. Nine times between 1095 and 1271, Christian armies set out to regain the Holy Land. Nine times they met defeat. But while the Crusaders failed in their religious mission, they did help to change the course of European economic history.

In the East the Crusaders discovered an unfamiliar and to them, fabulous, way of life. They wandered into bustling markets and watched people exchanging coins for consumer luxuries unheard of in Europe. They fingered soft, colorful silks. They ate strange foods seasoned with exotic spices. When it came time for them to retrace their steps westward, the Crusaders took samples of these marvels back with them.

The samples sparked European appetites for more of the same. It wasn't long before an east-west trade was flourishing. Silks and spices made their way to Italy, France, England, and Spain. Marketplaces reappeared in European towns and cities. Royal mints cranked up the production of coins. Borrowing and lending began anew.

Among the first to get into the lending business were those Crusaders who made up the order of the Knights Templar. The Templars were warriors who had dedicated their lives to the Christian Church, which in the western Europe of those days meant the Roman Catholic Church exclusively. As warriors, the Templars maintained fortified castles and plunged fearlessly into battle against the Muslim foe. As churchmen, they fasted, prayed, and obeyed strict religious laws.

Along with being churchmen and warriors, the Templars were guardians of wealth. Like members of other Catholic orders they received donations of gold, jewels, and other valuables. By the end of the twelfth century the Templars' headquarters in Paris, France, held one of the richest treasure troves in all Europe. At the height of their wealth and influence, the Templars employed seven thousand people. They owned 870 castles and houses from England to the Holy Land.

At first the Templars offered only rudimentary banking services. Members of the order in Paris accepted deposits of valuables from Crusaders bound for the Holy Land. When the Crusaders reached their destination, they went to one of the Templars' eastern strongholds and drew upon their deposits in local coins.[17] This system allowed Crusaders to have the use of their money while avoiding the nuisance and danger of transporting it themselves over long distances.

As the years passed, the Knights Templar began offering new services to their clients. In 1147 they loaned France's King Louis VII the money he needed to sponsor the Second Crusade. Forty years later the Templars assumed control of French financial affairs while King Philip II was off leading the Third Crusade. By the thirteenth century they were accepting deposits, holding mortgages, making loans, administering estates, and providing other banking conveniences to kings and princes across Europe. Like modern bankers, like the money changers of ancient Greece, the Templars charged fees for the services they rendered.

A QUESTION OF USURY

Those fees, however, were not considered usury because they did not profit the Templars as individuals. Everything the Templars earned was plowed right back into the order. Those earnings fed and clothed the Templars and went toward pursuing their goals in the Holy Land.

As devout Christians, the Templars would never have allowed themselves to profit personally from the loans they made. The Catholic Church's position against such profiting was absolute, based upon the Old Testament and the writings of Aristotle. Christians also remembered the New Testament story of how Jesus had scolded the money changers at the Temple in Jerusalem and had overthrown the tables upon which they displayed their wealth.[18] Both Church law and European secular (nonreligious) law prohibited the charging of interest.

The Templars' system of international banking—the world's first such system—fell apart early in the fourteenth century. In 1307, France's King Philip IV found himself desperate for money. Setting his sights on the Templars' immense treasure, he launched a vicious attack on the order. Within three years he had succeeded in destroying it. More than fifty of the order's leading members had been burned at the stake. The Knights Templars' wealth now belonged to Philip.

This was not the only atrocity Philip committed in his relentless pursuit of money. Earlier, in 1306, he had ordered his agents to seize the property of France's entire Jewish population. Then he drove the Jews from the kingdom empty-handed.[19]

Philip IV was just one of the European rulers who enriched himself in such a way. England's King Edward I had expelled his country's Jews and confiscated their property in 1290. Queen Isabella of Spain did likewise in 1492, the very year she saw the explorer Christopher Columbus off to the New World.

Destroying a Jewish community and seizing its goods was an easy road to riches for European monarchs, far easier than attacking a Christian order like the Knights Templar. Jews, after all, did not accept the Christian belief in Jesus as the Son of God. As unbelievers they were outside the protection of Church and secular law.

Outside the law's protection, certainly, but compelled nonetheless to obey it. And European rulers saw to it that the law, as it applied to the Jewish community, served their financial interests. By royal edict, Europe's Jews were forced into the role of moneylenders and usurers.

But doesn't Jewish law itself prohibit usury? Doesn't the Old Testament forbid the taking of interest? It does. Bear in mind, though, that while human beings have always felt uneasy about lending for profit, they know that as a practical matter, it must happen. People sometimes have to borrow, whether it's to fund a Crusade or feed a family. Yet no one, not even the ultra-scrupulous Knights Templar, can afford to lend strictly out of charity.

So the question for European kings and queens was this: How can I make sure that my subjects and I will be able to borrow when we need to, without any of us being forced into the sin of usury? Their answer was to exempt Jews from usury laws, giving them special permission to lend and collect interest. At the same time, Jews were legally barred from engaging in other trades or professions. That left moneylending as one of the few ways they could earn a living.

For Christians, this arrangement worked well. It ensured that they could get loans when they needed them without putting other Christians in moral jeopardy. And when a ruler needed extra income, as Philip IV had? Nothing simpler to do than to lash out at Jewish "unbelievers" and seize their "usurious" wealth.[20] In Islamic countries, incidentally, it was Christians who found themselves cast as the despised usurers. Christians committed the sin of profiting from lending while their Muslim customers remained faithful to the Koran.[21]

BANKERS AND PAWNBROKERS

Modern banking developed in northern Italy between the 1200s and the 1600s. The first "bankers" were money changers who sat at small benches in the marketplace, offering their services to merchants, traders, and travelers. Our word *bank* derives from the Italian word for "bench," *banco*. The English *bankrupt* comes from the same root. If a money changer failed and lost his wealth, his fellow money changers would smash his bench to pieces. This breakage, or rupturing, was a sign that the money changer was no longer able to conduct business.[22]

From traditional money changing to modern banking was no small transition. Before it could occur, bankers had to devise ways of getting around Europe's stringent usury laws. Among their most creative ideas was the "bill of exchange."

On the surface, a bill of exchange seemed to entail no more than an old-fashioned exchange of one kind of currency for another. A client would stop by a banco in the marketplace of an Italian city—Florence, say—and receive a sum of cash in local coins, florins. Client and banker would sign a bill of exchange.

According to the terms of the bill, the client agreed to repay the florins at a future time in a different kind of currency—a perfectly legal transaction. Suppose the repayment was to be in French francs. The client would pledge to deliver the francs to a designated person in a particular French city on a certain date. As was customary, the client would pay a fee for the privilege of exchanging one currency for another.

However—and here's the tricky bit—both banker and client understood that in reality their deal had nothing to do with money changing. No francs would be involved. There would be no trip to France or anywhere else. The client would repay the money—and the fee—in florins to the original banker in Florence. Disguised beneath all the fine language about francs and France and fees was an illegal, interest-bearing, for-profit loan.[23]

Ruses like this one allowed many an Italian family to prosper in banking. Most successful of all was the de' Medici family of Florence. The de' Medici began as bankers toward the end of the fourteenth century. As the family fortune grew, the de' Medici became great landowners and generous patrons of the arts. They were the friends—and creditors—of the richest and most powerful people across Europe. Yet although the de' Medici were famed as bankers to the wealthiest, they will forever be associated with those who lend to some of the world's poorest. The de' Medici coat of arms, the emblem of the family, consisted of three red balls against a black background. For centuries those three balls, altered to a golden hue, have identified pawnbroker shops around the globe.[24]

As "bankers to the poor," pawnbrokers drive a hard bargain. Whereas the de' Medici lent on trust, handing over large amounts of money to their rich clients on the strength of mere written documents, pawnbrokers extend credit only to those who have proved ahead of time that the debt will be repaid. That proof consists of some item of value—clothing, jewelry, a weapon. The client leaves the item with the pawnbroker—pawns it—as a condition of receiving the loan. The pawned item, called "collateral," is returned only when the loan is repaid.

For a pawnbroker, collateral represents security, which is why a pawnbroker's loan is of the type called "secured." A loan made on faith, a de' Medici loan for example, is an "unsecured" loan. If someone borrows from a pawnbroker and cannot make repayment within an agreed-upon amount of time, the pawnbroker keeps or sells the collateral. When that happens, the pawnbroker gets back the full amount of the loan—and then some. Pawnbrokers make a point of demanding collateral that is worth more than the loan. They also charge high rates of interest, anywhere from 24 percent to 240 percent in 1998.[25]

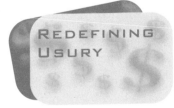

REDEFINING USURY

By the seventeenth century, the great Italian banking families had faded from the scene. All had failed, brought down by the reluctance or inability of European royalty to repay their loans.[26] But other lenders rose to take their place—

and to offer imaginative new banking services. In England those lenders included goldsmiths.

English goldsmiths had long been in the business of accepting deposits of valuables for safekeeping. They acknowledged deposits by giving each client a receipt indicating the exact worth of the goods or money left in their care. When a person with money on deposit wanted to buy something, he or she called on the goldsmith, produced a receipt, exchanged it for money, and went on to make the purchase.

Gradually, goldsmiths and their clients came to regard the receipts as being valuable in their own right. Each represented a specific amount of wealth. It was "as good as gold," so it could be used in place of gold. Now when a depositor wanted to buy merchandise, he or she would give a receipt directly to the seller. The seller would return the receipt to the goldsmith and receive payment. These goldsmiths' receipts, along with the Italian bankers' bills of exchange, were among the ancestors of our paper money.

England's goldsmiths were also responsible for introducing the forerunners of today's checks. A modern check is an order to a bank to pay a given sum to the individual or business whose name the check writer has filled in on the front of the check. The amount paid comes out of the check writer's bank account. The earliest "checks" were letters written by a goldsmith's clients. Clients would give the letters to their creditors, who would take—bear—them to the goldsmith. The goldsmith would pay each bearer the sum indicated in the letter.[27]

Innovations like "checks" and "paper money" were possible only because Europe had changed so much since the Dark Ages. Economically, life had been transformed. Business was booming. The consumer trade was flourishing as never before. Imports from the New World—gold and silver, furs and timber, fish and tobacco—were flooding into the Old World. The modern global economy was coming into being.

Ideas had changed, too. Once, Catholicism and its teachings had dominated western European thought. Now the Church had lost much of its authority. Religious protesters—Protestants—were challenging the old convictions with radical new beliefs of their own. Interest in secular education, virtually nonexistent since the fall of Rome, was rekindled. Schools and universities were founded.

With all the economic and intellectual changes, attitudes toward borrowing and lending were bound to change, too. Trade and business were the order of the day, and it was obvious that anyone who hoped to succeed had to have access to more money than most could raise without borrowing. The old proscriptions against lending for profit sounded out of place in such a commercial age. The Roman appreciation of the benefits of productive credit seemed increasingly relevant. "God did not forbid all profits so that a man can gain nothing," declared the Protestant leader John Calvin. "For what would be the result? We should have to abandon all trade in goods."[28]

Calvin was not alone in distinguishing between excessive interest rates and a lender's right to make a fair profit. His call for rethinking ancient assumptions about credit came in 1545. That same year, England repealed the laws that had defined usury as interest and banned it outright. New laws allowed, even encouraged, borrowing and lending. Maximum interest rates were established. During the next two hundred years, countries all over Europe copied England's example.[29] By the 1700s lending for profit was legal, legitimate, and commonplace.

The modern credit industry had started to take shape.

THREE

INVENTING THE CREDIT CARD

The first credit cards didn't look much like credit cards. They were made of paper, not plastic. They weren't cards either, but more like tiny booklets. Nor were the earliest cards anything like today's all-purpose passports to vast arrays of goods and services. They got their owners lunch or dinner in a dozen or so high-priced restaurants around New York City's Empire State Building. That was it.[1] Still, it was a start.

COLONISTS AND CREDIT

It should come as no surprise that the credit card would be invented in America. Americans have always felt comfortable using credit. That's partly because by the time North America began being colonized in the 1600s, Europeans were putting aside their old prejudices against borrowing and lending. The new European attitudes toward credit were reflected in laws and customs from Canada southward through New England to the mid-Atlantic colonies and beyond. Reminders of those colonial laws and customs survive today in the state and federal regulations that govern borrowing and lending.

Another reason Americans felt at ease with debt was that so many of them were themselves debtors. From the start,

Americans took full advantage of their credit opportunities. They borrowed to buy land, set up in business, travel west in search of valuable animal furs or precious metals—just about anything that seemed likely to help them get ahead.

Then there were those men and women who had made up their minds to go into debt in order to get to America in the first place. They were the colonies' indentured servants.

An indentured servant was someone who had signed a contract—papers of indenture—with another person who agreed to pay his or her way across the ocean. To repay the cost of the voyage, the indentured individual had to work, without salary, in the household of whomever had provided the transportation. Thousands of Europe's poor, hundreds still in their teens, arrived in America as indentured servants. After working off their debts (which typically took from five to ten years), many of the indentured prospered, becoming wealthy members of their communities.

Other colonists had simply stumbled into debt and as often happened in Europe, suffered terrible consequences.

During the seventeenth, eighteenth, and nineteenth centuries, it was legal to imprison people who ran up debts they could not pay. Debtors' prisons were frightful places. Whole families might be confined together, living in cold, cramped quarters with scant food and little in the way of sanitary facilities. The rule was that debtors could not work or earn money until they had made good on what they owed. Yet they were compelled to pay for their food and prison lodgings. In addition, their jailers demanded cash at every turn. Prisoners had to pay to have their iron shackles removed, for example. Even prison chaplains solicited bribes. Tens of thousands of debtors were to be found in prisons at any given time. They died by the score, often of starvation.[2]

In 1732 an English general, politician, and reformer named James Oglethorpe became interested in the plight of these unfortunates. He proposed that some be released and sent off to begin new lives in America. The plan won royal approval, and the next year, Oglethorpe and a small band of debtors founded the colony of Georgia. Land grants of up to 500 acres (202 hectares) in size were handed out.[3]

So that was colonial America. A haven for the destitute. A place in which few were strangers to debt. A land teeming with natural resources, whose traders and merchants had a keen appreciation of the benefits of "productive" credit. A land where no one hesitated to borrow if borrowing seemed the quickest route to riches.

CREDIT IN THE NINETEENTH CENTURY

By 1800 the United States had become an independent nation—with debt a way of life for many of its citizens. New York City pawnbrokers reported offering loans against 149,000 separate pieces of collateral in 1828[4]—this at a time when the city's total population hovered around 200,000![5] In rural areas too, borrowing was common. According to one later writer, nineteenth-century country people bought all manner of goods, "horses, plows, carriages, seed, clocks, and household furniture," on credit. Some borrowers pledged, like the Mesopotamian Puzurum nearly four thousand years earlier, to pay in full at harvest time. Others relied upon what was called open-book credit.

Open-book credit was most often used to purchase inexpensive everyday necessities such as food, clothing, farming supplies, and so on. A shopkeeper would allow customers to take home the goods they needed and pay their bills bit by bit, as they could afford to. Like those modern credit-card owners who pay part, but not all, of the balance due on their accounts each month, users of open-book credit generally owed some money. Yet relatively few ever fell into overwhelming debt. Both credit-card debt and open-book credit are classified as "revolving" credit because both consist of continuous cycles of borrowing and paying back.

Other early nineteenth-century merchants offered a nonrevolving type of credit: the installment plan. Installment plans were offered to well-to-do customers who planned to make an expensive one-time purchase on the order of a piano or an oriental carpet. This kind of purchase is referred to as "discretionary," since making it is up to the buyer's discretion, or judgment. Nondiscretionary purchases involve things people cannot do without—milk, a warm sweater, soap.

Installment buying calls for buyer and seller to sign a contract. Under its terms, the buyer makes an immediate, affordable, "down payment" on the item and takes it home. Then he or she makes smaller, regular payments until the item is entirely paid for and the debt is erased. In effect, an installment plan means that the seller lends the buyer the balance of a purchase's total cost.

From the buyer's point of view, installment buying can be a good deal. He or she has the use of the item being purchased and a reasonable amount of time in which to pay for it. Installment plans are good for sellers as well. They make it easier for customers to make discretionary purchases, thus promoting sales. They also protect the seller. The signed contract states that until an item is entirely paid for, the seller continues to own it. That makes an installment-plan sale a form of secured credit, with the item purchased serving as collateral for the loan. If the buyer fails to make payment, the seller can repossess the item. For the buyer, the threat of repossession is the downside of an installment plan.

Gradually, the nature of installment buying changed. Early in the nineteenth century it had been a way for the rich to acquire luxury goods. It was seen as a higher-class form of borrowing than the more common open-book credit. But by the century's end, installment buying had lost its cachet. Manufacturers of encyclopedias, mass-produced furniture, cheap jewelry, and other items hired sales agents to peddle their goods door-to-door, offering them to working-class families on the installment plan.[6]

Other credit schemes that targeted the poor were rent-to-own plans. Rent to own means exactly what it says. A customer agrees to rent an item, such as a household appliance, on a monthly basis for a specified amount of time. When the time is up the customer will own the item—assuming that no payments have been missed. Missing a payment can mean forfeiting the item. Rent-to-own deals come with enormous rates of interest built in. In 1998 a microwave oven that cost $140 in an appliance store cost close to $360 as a one-year rental purchase.[7]

The needy could also get credit through small-loan businesses. The first small-loan company opened in Chicago around 1870. It provided cash at exorbitantly high interest rates. Before long, similar outfits had sprung up around the country. Early in the twentieth century, lawmakers recognized the need to rein in the small-loan business. They did so by passing legislation that allowed the establishment of a new kind of lending institution, the credit union.

Credit unions are cooperatives. Members of a credit union pool their assets, then borrow from the pool when they need to. Credit union interest rates are generally about 1 or 1.5 percent a month.[8] The first credit union in North America was organized in Canada in 1900. By 1909 they were appearing around the United States.[9]

CHARGE CARDS AND AUTOMOBILES

Another early twentieth-century-credit novelty was the department store charge card.

Charge cards were first offered, as installment plans had been, to buyers of luxury goods. Upscale stores provided the cards to certain of their regular customers. Like early installment contracts, the cards benefited card owners and issuers alike. Owners were pleased to have been singled out for special treatment by their favorite department store. Only prized customers got charge cards. Besides, the cards were so convenient. Owning one meant not having to carry around large amounts of cash or go through the identification hassle involved in paying by check. A customer presented a store's card to a clerk, who recorded the sale. Once a month, the customer received a bill for thirty days' worth of purchases. The store charged nothing for this service. In return, the customer paid the bill in full each month.

Despite the expense of calculating bills and mailing them out, store owners also gained from this arrangement. The cards made it easy for merchants to keep track of purchases. More important, they boosted customer loyalty. People liked shopping in a store where they were treated as someone special. Above all, charge cards increased sales. Each was store specific, meaning that it could be used only in the store that had issued it. So each drew its owner back to that same store whenever he or she was in a spending mood.

The first decades of the twentieth century saw another development of major significance to the history of credit: growing automobile sales.

"The importance of the automobile in stimulating and legitimizing consumer credit sales cannot be overemphasized," says Lewis Mandell, author of *The Credit Card Industry: A History.* Mandell points out that autos were both necessary and expensive, essential to own, but too expensive for most people to buy as a single purchase. Rich, poor, and in-between, Americans bought their cars with credit.

"All social and economic classes were represented among the installment purchasers of automobiles," Mandell writes, "hence, installment buying acquired respectability." Buying on time was no longer associated with poverty as it had been just a few years earlier. That stigma had been removed.[10]

Another significance of autos was that they allowed people to cover long distances in a short time. An hour's travel could take drivers to places where they knew no one and no one knew them.

And then what if a car broke down? That happened a lot with early automobiles. Drivers could easily wind up far from home, in need of costly repairs, and without enough money to pay for them.

"To solve that problem," says Jack Weatherford, "...oil companies began issuing their own credit cards..." The cards could be used to buy company products—oil, gas, mechanical service—from anyone, anywhere, who sold those products.[11] Oil cards were unique. Unlike department store charge cards, they could be used to make purchases at thousands of locations around the country.

By the 1920s the makings of the modern credit card were at hand:

♦ Oil companies had shown that charge cards could be used on a nationwide basis.

♦ Automobile buying habits suggested that there was nothing shameful or inferior about buying on time.

♦ Americans had been enthusiastic users of credit for centuries.

All that remained to be done was to pull the elements together.

As it turned out, doing that took longer than might have been expected. The 1920s had been good years economically, but in 1929 financial disaster struck. Banks and businesses failed, not just in the United States and Canada but around the world. People lost their savings, their jobs, and their homes. Few were in the market for luxuries. Many could barely afford the necessities of life. Consumers continued to rely on open-book credit to pay for those necessities, but discretionary spending and installment sales of expensive goods dropped sharply. The Great Depression, as the economic crisis was called, lasted nearly a decade.

The Depression was not yet over in 1939 when World War II began in Europe. Canada entered the fighting at once, and the United States joined in two years later. Victory over Germany, Japan, and their allies came in 1945. With that, U.S. factories switched from the wartime production of guns, airplanes, and military uniforms to the manufacture of new cars, labor-saving appliances, sports equipment, and similar luxuries. Consumers prepared to go on an extended shopping spree. Within four years, some would be heading out the door credit card in hand.

The credit card as we know it was invented by three men over lunch in a New York City restaurant in 1949. Lewis Mandell describes the scene vividly. The three were convinced that there was money to be made in consumer credit. But how to tap into it? Department store charge accounts increased customer loyalty and stimulated sales, but since no interest was charged, the accounts were not in themselves a source of revenue. Installment sales produced interest, but that money went to cover the seller's expenses. It didn't make anyone rich.

What if, the three wondered, a third party inserted itself between buyer and seller? What if that third party promised business owners many new customers, customers they would not normally have attracted? What if that same third party offered affluent New Yorkers with good credit records a wide choice of establishments—not just one department store or one chain of gas stations—where they could charge purchases, no questions asked? Wouldn't those big spenders flock to the places of business that welcomed them as credit customers? And wouldn't business owners, seeing their profits soar, be willing to return a small percentage of those profits to the third party that had helped provide them? Wouldn't those small percentages add up to a fortune for that same third party—the three men themselves?

Excitedly, the three beckoned the restaurant's owner to their table. They had already decided that exclusive dining places like his would be exactly the right kind of business in which to test their money-making idea. What percentage would he give them for any credit-card business they sent his way? they asked. "Seven," he replied. The Diners Club was in business.

Early Diners Club cards really did resemble miniature books, says Lewis Mandell. Each displayed its owner's name on the front.[12] Inside were the names of the handful of New York City restaurants that had agreed to accept the cards. To begin with, owners paid nothing for their cards—no interest or annual fees. Participating restaurants handed over a percentage, or discount, of their Diners Club profits to the Club's three founding partners. The discount was, in accordance with the restaurateur's offhand suggestion, 7 percent.

The Diners Club grew rapidly. During its first month of operation, members charged $2,000 worth of meals and the partners took in $140. After less than half a year, charges had mounted to more than a quarter of a million dollars *a month*, and a Diners Club branch had opened in Los Angeles. Soon the company went international. In 1951 it showed its first profit, $61,222 on credit sales of more than $6 million.[13] Four years later the original paper cards were replaced with today's familiar plastic.[14]

Other changes were in the making. In 1950 the Diners Club had begun charging cardholders—now numbering 35,000—an annual $3 fee. Nearly three hundred businesses had signed on to the venture, and more would do the same. By the mid-1960s, not only restaurants but hotels, airline companies, retail shops, and the like were inviting customers to charge goods and services on their Diners Club cards. The Club's founders' dream of a "universal" card, one that could be used to purchase dozens of different kinds of items at hundreds of places around the world, was being realized.

In another change, this one aimed at encouraging more merchants to accept Diners Club cards, the Club adjusted its discount rate, lowering it in some cases to accommodate various business needs. Although restaurants continued to pay at the 7 percent rate, airlines were required to pay only 3 percent.[15] That seemed reasonable because airline tickets cost so much more than restaurant meals. Three percent of a $100 plane ticket earned the Diners Club $3, more than four times the 70¢ it made from 7 percent of a $10 dinner.

The Diners Club had its imitators. In 1958 the American Express company issued its own plastic credit card, and the Hilton Hotel chain introduced Carte Blanche. Carte Blanche and the Amex card, along with Diners Club, were categorized as travel and entertainment—T&E—cards. This was to distinguish them from another type of credit card, the bankcard.

Sensing that there were profits to be made in credit cards, banks had been edging into the field since the early 1950s. By 1955 more than one hundred U.S. banks were making cards available to their customers.

BANKCARD BLUES

For several reasons, these cards were not the quick moneymakers that T&E cards had been. To begin with, banks did not charge cardholders an annual fee. At first they did not even charge interest on unpaid balances. The banks' only source of income from their early credit cards was the discount each received from participating merchants. Those discounts did not amount to enough to cover the banks' credit-card operating expenses. Only when banks adopted a revolving type of credit, allowing credit-card customers to carry a balance from month to month—and charging interest—did the cards begin producing profits. For the majority of banks, the switch to revolving credit came in 1958 or 1959.

But other factors conspired to hold profits down. Many bankcard customers were in the habit of paying off their balances as soon as they came due. That may have been financially responsible, but from the banks' point of view it was bad news. Banks needed the interest income that was theirs only when customers availed themselves of a card's revolving credit feature. There was also the matter of fraud.

Some of the fraud was the banks' own fault. Unlike the T&E companies, banks mailed cards to potential customers without doing any checking up at all on their financial backgrounds. Cards went to people who were poor credit risks, already in debt, or just plain dishonest. Some of these people ran up thousands of dollars' worth of debt that the banks never recouped.

Other types of fraud were largely outside the banks' control. Thieves stole credit cards—clearly identifiable by the envelopes in which they came—from mailboxes. They picked up credit-card receipts from the wastebaskets and trash cans into which users had carelessly tossed them. The information on those receipts, which included cardholders' names and account numbers, allowed finders to run up huge bills they had no intention of paying. In 1966, U.S. banks lost $20 million to credit-card fraud. In 1970 fraud losses rose to $115.5 million.[16]

Also getting in the way of bankcard profitability was the fact that unlike the T&E companies, banks had no national distribution network. U.S. banks are regulated by federal law, and in the 1950s, 1960s, and 1970s, that law restricted interstate banking. The law has since been changed to allow banks greater freedom, but back then, each individual bank could issue cards only locally or within the state in which it was located.[17] As of 1958, the largest U.S. bankcard operation belonged to Bank of America, the nation's largest bank. That institution's BankAmericard could be used throughout California—but nowhere else.[18]

The bankcards' limited geographical usefulness made businesses reluctant to start accepting them. Business owners were afraid that so few of their customers would bother getting a card that any credit-card trade that did come their way would be offset by the discounts they would owe the bank. By the same token, consumers found that so few businesses would accept a bankcard that it was hardly worth applying for one. It was, as

Mandell puts it, a real chicken-or-egg situation.[19] Consumers hesitated to take a bank's credit-card offer because they couldn't use a card at most places of business, and businesses didn't want to become involved because not enough of their customers were cardholders. Bankcards went begging.

There was another reason merchants were reluctant to honor bankcards. Department stores had their own charge cards, which they had depended upon for decades to promote customer loyalty and increase sales. Stores were not about to risk alienating their best customers by allowing just anyone who happened to have a BankAmericard or a piece of Amex plastic to run up charges. America's "big three" retailers, Sears, J. C. Penney, and Montgomery Ward, were especially adamant in their refusal to go along with universal charge cards. In 1973 retail store cards still accounted for 54 percent of all U.S. credit cards. Bankcards accounted for just 11 percent.[20]

BANKCARDS TAKE OFF

With time, banks found ways to get more credit cards into circulation. In 1966, Bank of America announced it was setting up a national interchange that would enable banks all over the country to offer customers its BankAmericard. As Bank of America explained it, the system would work this way: Local banks would supply customers with BankAmericards, which they would use when they went shopping. Merchants from whom cardholders bought goods would report BankAmericard sales to their own local banks. Those banks would relay that information to all the banks of all the BankAmericard users who had made purchases. Cardholders would be billed through *their* local banks, and the merchants' banks would credit the cardholders' payments to the merchants' accounts. BankAmericards would be issued locally, as the law demanded. But thanks to the interchange, banks in every state would be able to offer their customers a BankAmericard that could be used anywhere in the country.

Bank of America's move took care of the credit-card distribution problem. It also prompted several other large banks to form a rival national credit-card network, the Interbank Card Association.[21] Interbank's card eventually evolved into Master Charge, and later, MasterCard. BankAmericard was renamed Visa. Yet even for what were to become two industry giants, profits remained elusive.

That changed with the 1980s. In April 1979, Visa announced that it had signed an agreement with the J. C. Penney department stores. From now on, Penney would accept Visa charges. Within three months, Sears had followed Penney's lead, signing up with both Visa and Master Charge. Today it is a rare business that does not display the Visa and MasterCard logos—along with those of several other credit-card companies—next to the cash register.

The Visa-Penney and MasterCard-Visa-Sears accords paved the way for increased profits for the two leading bankcard companies. It also forced local bank officials to acknowledge that they had lost control of the bankcards they themselves had pioneered. Theoretically, Visa and MasterCard were owned by the banks that offered their cards to customers. In reality though, the two had grown into powerful independent companies. Their independence was evidenced by the fact that under its agreement with Penney, Visa took its discount directly from the store chain. The local banks that had issued the Visa cards to J. C. Penney shoppers had no piece of that aspect of the financial action.[22]

The credit-card industry had come of age. And it was starting, finally, to make some real money.

FOUR

IN PURSUIT
OF PROFITS

Art Goldstein is not a careless person. He runs a successful business, a dating service, in Woodland Hills, California. He describes his credit history as "perfect." Goldstein uses credit cards, but explains that while he doesn't pay off his entire balance each month, he does pay more than the minimum due. He has never run up any sizable amount of credit-card debt. That's why he was so surprised to see the $45 interest charge on the credit-card bill that had just arrived in the mail.

Forty-five dollars in interest? Goldstein knew he hadn't charged an exceptionally large number of purchases over the previous thirty days. He also knew that the rate of interest he had been paying was low, just 6.9 percent a year. That low rate was the reason he had signed up for this particular card a few months earlier. Out of all the credit-card offers that had shown up in his mailbox—and plenty had—the 6.9 annual percentage rate (APR) deal was the best. How could he have racked up $45 worth of interest in a single month? Had he owed more than he thought he did? Made a mistake in writing out the check for his last payment? Forgotten to pay altogether?

The answer turned out to be none of the above. Scrutinizing his bill, Goldstein saw that his interest had jumped from 6.9 APR to a whopping 24.9 APR. "I was astounded," he says. "I didn't think that could be legal."

It was quite legal, as a few phone calls revealed. The 6.9 percent rate had been a special introductory rate, good for only the first few months he owned the card. Goldstein hadn't realized that. Thinking back, he did remember seeing the word "introductory" when he filled out the credit-card application, but he hadn't paid it much attention.

Nor had he focused on the printed notice that his credit-card issuer now informed him he had received five months later. That notice was meant to let Goldstein know that the introductory period was over and that his card's much higher regular APR was about to kick in. Goldstein hadn't given the notice a second glance. To him, it had appeared to be just one more bit of paper stuffed in among all the other flyers and ads that accompany any credit-card bill. He'd tossed it out with the other "junk." With that, he had legally committed himself to paying the steeper rate.

What happened to Art Goldstein isn't just legal, it's routine. Credit-card solicitations promise rates as low as 3.9 percent, 2.9 percent, even 1.9 percent, says Robert McKinley, president of RAM Research, a credit-card consulting firm. "But there is a lot of fine print," he adds. Once the introductory period is over, rates can go as high as 32.6 percent a year, McKinley cautions.[1]

From the beginning, companies that issue credit cards have manipulated interest rates, and the way they calculate interest, in order to maximize their income. We've already seen that in the late 1950s, banks adopted the revolving type of credit that allows—encourages—cardholders to remain perpetually in debt. At first banks used the "adjusted balance" method of figuring their credit-card customers' interest charges.

Under the adjusted balance system, finance charges are levied only on amounts of money that remain unpaid after they are due. Take a customer who charges $1,000 dollars' worth of merchandise on March 1. When her bill comes in at the end of the month she pays only $100 out of the $1,000 she owes. The other $900 remains outstanding. At this point her credit-card issuer starts charging her interest on that $900. If her annual interest rate is 24 percent, her monthly rate will be one twelfth of that, or 2 percent. The customer will see an $18 interest charge on her next bill.

During the 1970s, banks and other credit-card issuers changed from the adjusted balance system to the "average daily balance" system. Using average daily balance, creditors charge interest from the date of the purchase, rather than from the date payment is due. And unless the bill is paid in full on its due date, they charge interest on the entire amount of the bill, not just on any balance that remains outstanding.

What did the change imply for credit-card users? "In the extreme case," explains Lewis Mandell, "a customer who charged $1,000 on the first day of the payment period and repaid all but a penny of that sum on the due date...would be assessed full interest on the $1,000 for the entire month." At 2 percent monthly, that would be a $20 charge on 1¢ owed. So extreme an example is improbable in real life. Nevertheless, Mandell tells us that the bankcard issuers of the 1950s figured they could raise their revenues between 15 and 25 percent by moving to the average daily balance system.[2] Under this system the woman who pays only $100 of her $1,000 bill will see her one-month interest charge rise from $18 to $20. A small dollar increase, but enough to raise a bank's credit-card profits by that 15 to 25 percent.

Credit-card issuers are still finding new ways to raise their interest-related income. One recent change has been to charge varying rates of interest based upon a cardholder's individual credit record. Cardholders who regularly pay the minimum due on time are charged a relatively low rate of interest, 13 percent annually, perhaps. Cardholders with a history of missing payments may have to pay from 20 to 30 percent or more a year.

Another maneuver has been to fiddle with what is known as the "grace period." The grace period is the time between the date of a purchase and the date payment is due. At first, that period was thirty days, corresponding to the normal monthly billing cycle. Cardholders who paid their bills in full within the thirty-day grace period were charged no interest. By the 1990s the grace period for many cardholders had shrunk to twenty-five days. As the decade ended it was shrinking again, this time to twenty days.[3]

What does a reduced grace period mean? That finance charges can start piling up even before a cardholder's bill arrives in the mail. Suppose you make a $10 purchase with a credit card on November 1. Suppose further that the card bears an interest rate of 2 percent monthly and has a twenty-day grace period. By the time you receive your bill on November 30, you already owe ten days' worth of interest, or about 6.7¢. That isn't much, and you'll probably pay it without thinking twice. But look at that reduced grace period from an issuer's perspective. Six hundred million Visa cards were in circulation in 1998.[4] What did Visa issuers stand to make from 600 million times 6.7¢? Look at the figures again from your own point of view. What if you had charged $100 worth of goods instead of $10 worth and paid 2 percent interest for 10 days? What if you had charged a really expensive item like a computer?

Of course consumers are not helpless when it comes to interest charges and reduced grace periods. The best way to avoid being stung by either—or at least to keep costs to a minimum—is to pay bills promptly. It is also important to shop around for good deals. Fixed, nonintroductory APRs of as low as 9.9 percent were available in 1998.[5] But be aware that a "fixed" rate stays fixed at a given level only until a company decides to refix it at a different rate. Another possibility is to sign up for a credit card with a low introductory rate, use it until the rate goes up, then drop it in favor of a new card and a new special rate. This guerrilla tactic can be either sort of fun or a pain in the neck, depending upon one's mind-set. How many of us would bother to follow through and switch cards every few months?

THE FEES SQUEEZE

In the early years credit-card fees were few and far between. Those that were in place were low. The first bankcards were free and T&E cards cost just a few dollars a year. Transaction fees were rare.

All that has changed. Service fees are soaring, and bankcard annual fees are increasingly common. It costs $125 a year to carry a Citibank Platinum Select AAdvantage card, for instance. One American Express card bears an annual fee of $300.[6] It's true that prices for nearly everything have risen since the 1950s, but credit-card fees have escalated beyond recognition. They rose 17 percent in 1997 alone, according to one expert.[7]

What does a Citibank Platinum Select AAdvantage cardholder get for $125 a year? The card's name hints at the answer—unlimited free mileage on American Airlines. Offering credit-card users free mileage based upon how much they charge—the more they charge the more miles they "earn"—is common in the industry. Most issuers, however, limit the number of free miles each cardholder can accumulate. The $125 Citibank card, on the other hand, has no limit. American Express's $300-annual-fee card also lets users earn free air miles. Besides that, it allows travelers to "upgrade," to buy economy class airline seats, for example, then to exchange them for business or first-class seats at no extra charge. Another of the card's perks is the opportunity to meet a celebrity entertainer backstage after a concert or theater performance.[8]

Not every cardholder is willing to fork over $300 a year for the privilege of meeting a celebrity—presumably as one of a horde of other cardholders doing the exact same thing—or to pay $125 to obtain unlimited free miles. (Later in this chapter we'll see how restrictive such mileage programs can be.) Fortunately for the frugal, dozens of available cards carry no annual fees.

Unfortunately for the frugal and for everyone else, most no-annual-fee cards carry a host of other charges. Stephanie Gallagher, writing in *Kiplinger's Personal Finance Magazine*, lists them: "maintenance fees, late fees, convenience-check fees...Fees to process applications for new accounts and fees to close old accounts. Inactivity fees when we don't use our cards enough and over-the-limit fees when we use them too much."[9]

Fees aren't just numerous—they're hefty. In 1996 the very highest credit-card late-payment fee—the penalty for not paying the minimum due on time—was $18. By early 1998 late-payment fees were typically $25, and before the year ended some had hit the $29 level. That is a 61 percent increase in under three years. It is worth noting, by the way, that late payments are not necessarily the result of negligence or an inability to pay. An unexpected trip out of town, a family illness, a storm that interferes with mail delivery—any untoward event can delay payment and trigger a penalty.

Automated Teller Machine (ATM) fees are another source of income for credit-card issuers. "The cash-advance business is a tremendous service," says Spencer Nilson, publisher of *The Nilson Report*, a credit-card industry newsletter based in California. Indeed it is. With an ATM card a person can get money just about anywhere at any time—in an emergency, during a visit to a foreign country, or when banks and stores are closed. However, Nilson warns, ATM card issuers "can charge you anything they want." One Cincinnati, Ohio, bank places a minimum $20 fee on every cash advance. Add to that the interest charged on money withdrawn and an ATM user can wind up paying what is in effect a 40 percent rate of interest.[10]

An outrageous rate, but at least those who incur it do so while taking advantage of a valuable service. But what about cardholders forced to pay for *not* having used a particular service, such as a card's revolving credit feature? Cardholders who do not use the feature, who pay their bills in full each month, are called convenience users. Convenience users do not carry cards in order to obtain credit to buy items they could not otherwise afford. They carry them because the cards make shopping so simple. Present the plastic, scrawl a signature, and that's it.

Credit-card companies, however, frown on convenience users precisely because they do not go into debt and end up paying interest. Although issuers do not want cardholders to skip payments or fall into unmanageable debt, neither do they like to see them getting away with owing no interest whatsoever. That is why the financial branch of the General Electric Corporation, for example, charges the convenience users of its GE Rewards MasterCard $25 a year. Fining convenience cardholders for not going into debt makes up to some extent for what they cost GE in loss of interest income. People who own cards but fail to use them often enough may be penalized as well. Mellon Bank of Pittsburgh, Pennsylvania, slaps a $15 fee on its credit-card customers every time they go six months without ringing up a charge.[11]

Fees charged to open or close a credit-card account also help boost income. Opening fees are particularly steep among companies that cater to people whose history of debt makes it hard for them to obtain credit, Stephanie Gallagher says. Delaware-based Cross Country Bank demands a $100 application processing fee in addition to a $50 annual fee on its Visa card. The Visa Future Card has a one-time $70 "set-up" fee, a one-time $98 "program" fee, and an ongoing $5 monthly "participation" fee.[12] Start-up and shut-down fees on other cards are lower but they, too, contribute to proceeds. At the same time these particular fees seem liable to put a halt to the habit some cardholders have of hopping from one low introductory rate program to another, switching accounts just ahead of higher regular APRs.

To illustrate the effect a combination of high interest rates and automatic penalties can have on credit-card users, a public-interest group called Consumer Action offers this hypothetical example:

> A cardholder has a $2,000 balance. He pays only the minimum 2 percent due each month and makes late payments in the second and third monthly billing cycles. He is assessed two late-payment fees—$25 each—and his interest rate is upped from 13 percent to 24 percent. In the sixth month he misses yet another payment and is charged an additional $25. Over half a year, the cardholder has paid $277 in interest and late fees. His $2,000 balance has grown to $2,076.

In Consumer Action's scenario, the unlucky cardholder is locked into this dismal situation:

> As long as the cardholder's interest rate remains at 24 percent and he pays only 2 percent of his balance, or about $40 a month, his payments will almost exactly equal the minimum due. He will never reduce his original debt. The payments he makes will never cover more than finance charges and fees.[13]

Although being permanently trapped in such a fashion is highly unlikely, millions of borrowers do find themselves paying back far more money than they ever took out in loans. That is what the credit industry is all about.

Credit is a commodity, like any other. It has a value of its own, just as rice has or gold or the hunting licenses the Russian government was handing out to workers in the late 1990s. Credit's value lies in the fact that it allows people to gain the immediate use or possession of something they cannot afford to pay for outright. Lenders sell credit, much as grocers sell bananas. Borrowers buy credit, purchasing it with interest and fees. And the more they need credit, the more they are willing to spend to get it, which is why even such ultra-expensive cards as Visa Future and Cross Country Bank Visa find ready takers.

OTHER SOURCES OF INCOME

Credit-card companies also make money by delivering customers to retailers. We've seen that the Diners Club's original flat 7 percent discount was quickly replaced with a more flexible system that allowed lower discounts to providers of some high-priced goods and services. Discount rates continued to drop as card companies sought to entice more and more merchants to join their networks. Between 1990 and 1998, American Express lowered its discount from 3.22 percent to 2.74 percent. Visa claims to average under 2 percent. Visa's nearly full percentage point lower rate, industry analysts say, helps explain why Visa cards are accepted by more than 14 million businesses worldwide, while only five million accept Amex.[14]

Another money-maker for card issuers is so-called cross-selling. Cross-selling—advertising—accounts for all those "stuffers" whose abundance led Art Goldstein to overlook the notice about his interest rate hike.

Some cross-selling involves an issuer's own products. One couple's KeyBank MasterCard bill comes with an ad for a Key home-equity loan printed across the bottom. Home-equity loans allow homeowners to borrow using their homes as collateral. The KeyBank cardholding couple is being urged to apply to the bank for thousands of dollars in new loans. A Visa platinum bill invites a young Brooklyn, New York, woman to "write her own check" for a cash advance. The blank check is right there, attached to her bill. All the woman has to do is to fill in her name and the amount she wants—up to $4,811, the amount of credit in her Visa account—and the money is hers. (If she isn't going to use the check, though, she would be well advised to destroy it. Anyone can sign the woman's name on the check—it's printed, along with her address, right on the front—and tap into her credit account.) Banks also offer credit-card insurance; if a cardholder dies owing on his or her account, the insurance pays off the debt. The more products credit-card lenders can convince their customers to buy, and the more debt they accumulate, the greater the lenders' potential income.

Cross-selling can also involve other companies' products. By the 1970s, ads for goods as diverse as fire extinguishers, cooking utensils, tape recorders, coin collections, handheld calculators, and radios were filling bankcard billing envelopes, says Lewis Mandell. Banks took a 15 percent discount on every item sold.[15] Today's credit-card bills come with ads for everything from stamp collections to roadside auto repair service to theater tickets.

Cross-selling, retailer discounts, and interest and fee charges to cardholders combined to push credit-card profits higher and higher in the early and mid-1980s. But by the 1990s, the industry found to its dismay that profits were beginning to lag. In 1996 they plummeted 24 percent. The next year, overall profits remained flat.[16]

FINANCIAL WOES

Why the drop-off? Part of the answer has to do with the country's soaring personal bankruptcy rate. The 1.3 million Americans who filed for bankruptcy in 1997 constituted a record-breaking number for the seventh year in a row. And people don't go into bankruptcy because they owe a few hundred dollars—they do it because they owe tens or hundreds of thousands, much of it on their credit cards. Under U.S. law as it stood in 1998, individuals who declared legal bankruptcy did not have to repay their credit-card debts. Analysts estimated that the industry was losing over $12 billion a year due to bankruptcies.[17]

Losses due to fraud, on the other hand, are no longer the

major concern they were when the credit-card industry was new. Not that attempts at fraud are unknown. In one 1998 case, the owner-chef of a top New York City restaurant was charged with padding his customers' bills. The fraud was not subtle; the restaurant owner had allegedly written in "tips" of up to $30,000 onto diners' credit-card slips. According to the company that processed the restaurant's credit charges, the owner managed to steal $190,000 before being caught.

But catching him was pretty much a matter of routine, company officials hasten to add. Sophisticated electronic equipment, available since the mid-1990s, makes it easy to detect cheating. "[T]hey're able to analyze millions of transactions and find patterns of fraud fairly quickly," David Robertson, president of *The Nilson Report*, says of the new devices. "It's quite a success story, actually."

Few would disagree. Fraudulent charges, as well as charges that customers dispute and which may or may not involve fraud, are called "charge backs" in the credit-card business. One Visa vice president points out that in 1990 he was seeing a charge-back rate of 0.28 percent. That amounted to 4.9 million disputes on $1.89 billion in business. By 1998 the rate had dropped to 0.06 percent—4.5 million disputes on $6.8 billion worth of transactions. "As an industry, we've seen a dramatic reduction in charge-back rates over the last eight years," he says.[18]

Overshadowing fraud as a reason for diminished credit-card profits, experts maintain, is something for which card issuers can blame only themselves. They have promoted their products foolishly.

Throughout the 1990s issuers introduced one new gimmick after another, all aimed at attracting new customers. They offered free airline miles and travel upgrades. They offered low introductory rates. One offer from the Travelers Group went so far as to include a zero percent starter rate. Companies offered increasing numbers of "prestige cards" named after rare and precious metals—gold, platinum, titanium. Gold cards carried more perks than regular cards—more free miles, automatic insurance coverage on rented cars, or higher lines of credit. Platinum cards claimed to offer more benefits then gold ones (naturally, since platinum is about four times as expensive as gold), and titanium cards (a form of the element titanium is what puts the starry sparkle in some sapphires and rubies) still more. American Express offered "special treatment at your favorite stores" and "a complimentary ride home from the airport when you've been traveling" to new cardholders. Diners Club promised free hotel stays and what it described as vacation packages. "Rebate card" offers invited people to apply for the cards, use them to charge purchases—and get back a portion of what they spent.

Rebates? Free hotel stays? Zero interest rates? No wonder profits were down. "The credit-card free-for-all has come back to haunt the industry," Robert McKinley says.

It's haunting credit-card users as well. The drop in profits is one reason for all the punitive new credit-card fees, reduced grace periods, and higher interest rates, McKinley asserts.[19] Credit-card issuers need all the income they can get. Lower profits are also the reason card issuers have launched massive selling campaigns aimed at signing up millions of new cardholders. Especially young ones.

PROMOTING DEBT

"Cool Shoppin' Barbie" is part of one of those campaigns. The doll appeared in toy stores just in time for the 1997 holiday shopping season. Designed for children as young as three, Cool Shoppin' Barbie comes with boutique-style clothes, a battery-powered cash register and credit-card scanner—and her very own MasterCard. Swipe the card through the scanner and, "Credit approved!" Barbie exclaims.

Why a play MasterCard for preschoolers? "Obviously, MasterCard is trying to establish brand identity at a young age," says Gerri Detweiler, author of *The Ultimate Credit Handbook*. Research uniformly shows that over the years cardholders remain most loyal to the first type of card they ever owned. People who started out with MasterCard pull out their MasterCards more often than any other brand of card they also happen to carry. Those who initially signed up with Visa tend to stick with Visa. Cool Shoppin' Barbie represents MasterCard's way of trying to get a jump on the competition in 2012. That's the year 1997's three-year-olds will turn eighteen and become legally old enough to own a credit card.[20]

Don't assume, though, that other credit-card issuers are standing idly by watching MasterCard corner the youth market. Far from being idle, they're busy bombarding young people with advertising for their own products.

Nathan Morrison was a college junior when he received a Visa card application from Associates National Bank. "Free from parental rule at last," trumpeted the envelope's boldface type. "Now all you need is money."[21] Nathan could only agree.

"You're among the first to be invited to apply for the new First USA Titanium MasterCard," a letter informed one full-time graduate school student. The student was flattered—First USA was offering her a card with a credit line of "up to $100,000." A Massachusetts girl who wants to be known only as Jeannie was hardly out of high school when she heard from a soon-to-be fellow college student urging her to apply for a credit card. A parent identified as "M. M." of Boise, Idaho, wrote to the magazine *Consumer Reports* to complain about a Visa Gold card offer made to a seven-year-old daughter. Was this desperation on Visa's part—or just carelessness?, M. M. wanted to know.

Probably a little of both, was *Consumer Reports'* answer.[22] Of course a seven-year-old would hardly qualify for a credit card even with an adult cosigner. But credit-card companies are passionate in their eagerness to sign up new customers. They mailed three billion credit-card applications to Americans in 1998.[23] It is hardly surprising if a few were misdirected. Credit-card companies also solicit prospective cardholders by telephone. They advertise in newspapers and magazines, via flyers and brochures, on campus bulletin boards and city buses, over the Internet, in banks and other places of business—just about everywhere imaginable.

The ads seem to be having the desired effect. According to a 1998 survey, 55 percent of U.S. college students applied for and got credit cards in their freshman year. Twenty-five percent arrived on campus with cards they had acquired in high school.[24]

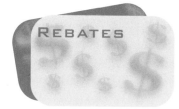

How good are the new credit-card offers? The Visa solicitation that went to Nathan Morrison promised no annual fee, a card that would entitle him to fifteen minutes of free telephone time, and—best of all—a 3 percent rebate on purchases made with the card.

Wait a minute, though. Nathan peered at the fine print, "You earn a...rebate...during each billing cycle in which the total of payments and credits to your account is less than the previous balance." Nathan understood that to mean that he would get 3 percent back on charges *only* if he used the card's revolving credit feature and paid interest on his balance each month. "Incredibly preposterous," was his reaction. The way Nathan figured it, if he charged $3,333 a year on the card and kept a running balance of $420 a month on which he paid interest, that interest would exactly equal the amount of his rebate.[25]

Not all rebate cards are bad deals, says Stephanie Gallagher. She recommends supermarket chain credit cards that offer rebates of up to 3 percent on purchases made in stores in the chain and 1 percent on purchases elsewhere. But some rebate cards "aren't worth the plastic they're printed on," she adds. Gallagher and others remind us that virtually all rebate cards carry higher interest rates than regular cards.[26] It's also important to remember that the terms of rebate cards—and other cards as well—are constantly changing. Checking the fine print is essential when applying for a card. Equally essential is to keep on checking with each new bill.

Other credit-card come-ons can be as iffy as the one Nathan Morrison received. An Augusta, Maine, lawyer signed on for a platinum card that promised one free airline mile for every dollar he charged. On his second bill he discovered a $35 fee—the cost of the "free" mileage program. He protested to the card's issuer but to no avail. No $35—no free miles. He paid up. Less than two weeks later, the lawyer was notified by letter that the terms of the program had changed again. From now on, as a convenience user, he would be getting *half* a mile for every dollar he charged. Only if he carried an interest-bearing balance would he get the whole mile for each dollar spent. "Guess what," the lawyer fumed in print. "The card that I had paid $35 for, which I didn't think I had to pay anything for, now only will give me one half of the miles for every dollar I spend if I don't pay interest on the account."[27] It's not that there is necessarily anything wrong with this platinum card as a credit card. Using it to earn airline miles could be an expensive way to fly, however.

Citibank's regular AAdvantage card costs its frequent fliers as well. "You would need to charge $25,000 within three years to earn a round-trip economy ticket within the continental U.S. on American Airlines," says *Money* magazine. Assuming an AAdvantage cardholder flew economy from New York City to Los Angeles and back—$341 in 1997—that person had earned 1.4¢ for every dollar charged. How much of a bargain is that?

A lot of rebate cardholders don't do even that well out of their cards. In 1997 about one in four credit cards in use in the United States was a rebate card. However, only half of rebate-card customers actually collected the rewards they were owed that year.[28] The other half paid fees and high interest rates—and got nothing in return.

PRESTIGE CARDS

Prestige cards—gold, platinum, and titanium—may not be all they're cracked up to be either. Such cards are useful, of course, and many offer perfectly good deals. But each claims to be unique, to offer better terms and more perks than any other card on the market. Such claims are questionable. "Little really differentiates these pieces of plastic," warns *Consumer Reports.* The magazine's editors note that while First USA's titanium card touts its discounts on purchases from 2,500 retailers, some of the bank's platinum cards offer similar discounts.[29]

There is a reason issuers push consumers to add platinum and titanium cards to the regular and gold cards already in their wallets. They all want to sell more cards. "IMPORTANT," says a notice that went to one man along with the offer of a Citibank Platinum Select MasterCard. Already the owner of two MasterCards, KeyBank Gold and Chase Manhattan GrandElite, this man is being urged to add a third to his collection. "Do not hesitate to accept this card just because you already carry another MasterCard," the notice goes on. "Your new Citibank Platinum Select card will carry its own separate line of credit." And platinum *is* more valuable—and hence more exclusive-sounding—than gold. Perhaps this man can be persuaded he will feel richer or more important with a platinum card. "This is a very inexpensive way to get you to change banks—over the color of the card," says Robert McKinley.

Prestige cards also try to snare new customers with generous line-of-credit offers. Take those offers with a grain of salt, experts advise. Is First USA really going to give a full-time graduate student with a part-time job $100,000 worth of credit? "Only a small number of cardholders—typically those with high incomes and sterling credit histories—will qualify" for such a high line of credit, answers Margaret Mannix in *U.S. News & World Report* magazine.[30] Far more realistic for that student was the offer she received from American Express: $5,000 in credit to be paid back in sixty monthly installments of $116.08 each. What is more, even if she wanted to pay $1,964.93 for the privilege of borrowing $5,000, Amex might not let her. The fine print stipulates that the $5,000 loan offer is good only for those earning $25,000 or more a year. Far from being able to borrow $100,000 as First USA suggests, this student may not be able to lay her hands on a measly $5,000.

Then again, she may. Credit-card issuers urge college students to count as "personal income" the education loans they have received as well as any allowance they may get from their parents. According to a Maryland bankruptcy lawyer, some even count as assets the credit available to them on charge cards.[31] "By that measure," says financial writer Jane Bryant Quinn, "[a student's] 'income' could be $20,000 or more—allowing for a lot of debt." And young people can get into that debt without their parents being aware it's happening. People age eighteen and up do not need parental permission to own a credit card—or three or four. "You'll never know [they're in debt]," Quinn warns parents, "until the tearful phone call home."[32]

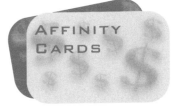
AFFINITY CARDS

Another marketing ploy revolves around what are called affinity cards. Affinity cards are designed to appeal to the special tastes, interests, hobbies, and personal backgrounds of potential cardholders. A woman who belongs to The Nature Conservancy, a group that works to protect the environment, receives a Nature Conservancy Platinum Plus card application. The cards pictured on the accompanying flyer display The Nature Conservancy name and logo, along with a choice of appealing animal portraits. The woman's husband, who subscribes to *The Nation*, a current-affairs magazine, gets an ad for *The Nation* Visa card. Other affinity cards are aimed at golfers, coffee lovers,

Italian Americans, New Yorkers, college graduates, you name it. There is even a card especially for middle-aged people who may be losing the ability to read small print—the Chase LensCard with built-in magnifying lens. The giant affinity card company MBNA boasted a network of 4,600 sponsoring organizations and card-issuing banks and other financial institutions in 1997.[33]

The affinity-card sales pitch is multifaceted. First, the cards are advertised as being good deals in themselves. Features typically include no annual fees, low introductory rates, and all the rest. Second, affinity cards convey a level of prestige beyond associations with mere precious metals. Who wouldn't want to flash a card that proclaims its user a caring, compassionate defender of wildlife? Or one that links its owner to a prestigious university famed for its brilliant students and faculty? What golfer wouldn't want to be identified with his favorite sport, or Italian American with her proud heritage? Americans have never been shy about broadcasting their individual opinions and preferences. Just look at all the T-shirt slogans and automobile bumper stickers and vanity license plates on public display. Affinity-card issuers win new customers by offering them one more way to tell the world what they believe in and feel strongly about.

A third selling point for some affinity cards is that they give cardholders the opportunity to support a favorite cause or institution every time they use the cards to charge purchases. Take the Land for Maine's Future cards, issued by MBNA in conjunction with the state of Maine. People who carry those cards—each decorated with a picturesque Maine scene—have the satisfaction of knowing that 0.5 percent of the amount they charge goes into a special Maine state government fund. In future years, that fund will be used to buy land to be set aside for conservation or public recreation. Other affinity cards earn revenues for such organizations as the Make-A-Wish Foundation, which provides gifts and trips for youngsters with serious illnesses; Reading Is Fundamental, the child literacy project; and the Smithsonian

Institution, the museum and research and education center in Washington, D.C.

Like other types of credit cards, affinity cards have their pluses and minuses. It's nice to think that part of the cost of that new backpack or computer is going toward a good cause, but how much money is actually involved? Users of the MBNA Land for Maine's Future card were expected to charge enough to raise $50,000 for the state's land-buying fund in the program's first year and another $75,000 in its second. By the start of the twenty-first century, it was estimated, the fund would have reached the $500,000 mark. In fact, only $43,000 was raised in the first two years. That amount of money would just about pay for a single waterfront house lot in the 1999 real estate market.[34] Maybe it would be better for the state's conservation-minded residents to donate directly to the land-preservation fund of their choice and pick their credit cards based strictly on each one's financial merits. Even participating in a nationwide revenue-sharing program, which can be expected to raise more than a state undertaking, can be an expensive way to donate to a charity or other cause. If consumers paid cash for purchases instead of charging them and donated the interest money saved thereby, charities might come out ahead.

There is another consideration as well. Just because an affinity card's cause seems attractive does not mean the card itself is worth bothering with. Look at *The Nation* Visa. That card might be expected to offer users unusually favorable terms. *The Nation* advertises itself as a progressive magazine, one that is concerned about the "little guy" as opposed to "big business." It is a magazine whose writers and editors generally express less sympathy toward lenders and their complaints about rising bankruptcy rates than toward borrowers angered by high interest rates and mounting fees.

Yet the card that bears *The Nation* name is no different from most other cards. It hits users with a punitive 22.99 percent interest rate after two missed payments within a six-month period. Ads for the card also include that misleading "Credit Line Up To $100,000" headline. Only in print almost too small to read do the words "In certain instances, you may receive a Classic card with a credit line up to $5,000," appear. It's a good bet that "certain" means "most" in this case. Other fine-print warnings in *The Nation* Visa ads include information about fees for ATM cash advances, transaction fees for money orders, and the like. The bottom line is that this card, like the Land for Maine's Future card, or a card that allows users to donate to the Smithsonian or Reading Is Fundamental, or a prestige or rebate card, is simply a credit card. Its purpose is exactly the same as that of every other credit card—to turn a profit for the industry.

But no credit card can do that unless we consumers do our part as well and spend, spend, spend.

FIVE
WHEN
C-R-E-D-I-T
SPELLS
TROUBLE

There are approximately 100 million households in the United States. A household is defined as a person or people inhabiting a single dwelling. A mother and her baby living in an apartment make up a household. So do a married couple in a mansion with their four children and live-in nanny. So does a teenager who lives on his own and supports himself.

Of U.S. households, 80 percent contained at least one credit card in 1998. Most contained more—eleven on average.

Less than one third of 1998's U.S. cardholding households were free of credit-card debt that year. The majority, 69 percent, were carrying a balance—an average of $7,000—from month to month. That figure did not include other types of household debt, home mortgages, car and education loans, money borrowed from friends or family, and the like.

In 1994, 1.66 percent of U.S. borrowers were delinquent, meaning that they were not only in debt but had fallen behind in making payments on what they owed. Three years later, despite a booming national economy, the delinquent percentage had risen to 2.55.[1]

Other unsettling statistics come from the nation's college campuses. Sixty-seven percent of U.S. college students owned at least one credit card in 1998. Twenty-seven percent had four or more. Average college student credit-card debt amounted to $1,879. Seven percent of students owed more than $7,000 in noneducation debt. In 1997, 32 percent of American college students were paying $1,000 or more a month to cover credit-card debt, compared to only 10 percent six years earlier.[2]

Finally, over 1.3 million individual Americans were forced to declare bankruptcy in 1997. That was eight times the personal bankruptcy rate the country saw during the Great Depression of the 1930s.[3] "The trend is credit-card debt is up and bankruptcy is up," says an assistant to one New York State lawmaker. "There's more than a casual relationship here."[4] Yet it is people in those households *without* cards who are likely to face the most devastating credit problems of all. That is because few Americans are without credit cards out of choice. In general, not having a card is a sign of past bankruptcy or other financial difficulty.

For too many Americans, credit definitely spells trouble.

It's not hard to run into credit trouble. People can do it through no fault of their own, without even being aware that anything has gone wrong.

One woman realized she was in trouble only when she began receiving phone calls from a collection agency. According to the calls, which came from early in the morning until late at night, the woman owed over $500 on a department-store charge account. If she didn't pay the minimum $125 due immediately, she was told, she would be assessed a penalty.

There was some mistake, the woman protested. She had charged about $100 worth of goods at a local branch of the store in the previous month and that was all. As was her legal right, she asked for a copy of her account. It showed that the disputed charges were for purchases she would never have made at a store branch in a state she had never visited. The woman tried explaining that to the collection agency callers, but none would listen. Time after time the callers interrupted her, rudely demanding payment. At last the woman resorted to writing letters to company headquarters. Even then it took store employees two months to track down the mistake, correct it, and put an end to the harassing calls.

Mistakes like this one are not uncommon and they can happen to anyone. Thomas Galvin is a leading New York City investor, a prominent businessman who regularly treats clients to lunch or dinner at posh Manhattan restaurants. It was after one such meal that Galvin handed his American Express card to a waiter, only to have it politely rejected. Galvin was not entirely surprised. Weeks earlier he had received a letter from Amex informing him that his card had been canceled because "of our receiving notification of your filing bankruptcy." In reality, Galvin was about as far from bankruptcy as it is possible to be. The letter was the result of a computer error. Galvin had gotten in touch with American Express, pointed out the mistake, and assumed the matter had been cleared up. It had not.

Galvin, evidently a good-humored man, was sufficiently amused by Amex's letter to have it framed and hung on his office wall.[5] But not everyone can afford to laugh off credit errors. The woman hounded by collection-agency phone calls felt genuinely threatened. As far as she was concerned, a blot on her otherwise excellent credit record would have been no laughing matter. And what about the many Americans who depend upon credit cards to pay their regular monthly bills—rent, electricity, gas, telephone? How can they make payments if a card is mistakenly canceled? They can't—and that may mean piling real delinquency on top of someone else's goof.

Or what if a computer glitch makes it appear that a cardholder has missed a payment? He or she will be charged a penalty fee and may have to start paying a higher rate of interest, typically from 20 to 30 percent annually. With a 24 percent APR, a cardholder with an average $7,000 balance could be paying $140 a month in interest. True, most mistakes are eventually corrected. Wrongly imposed fees and interest charges can be refunded. In the short run though, a person burdened by debt or scraping along on a limited income can face real trouble when errors occur.

MORE
TROUBLE

In what other ways can responsible credit-card owners get into trouble? Perhaps surprisingly, one answer is *not* when a card gets lost or stolen. Laws protect cardholders against liability for fraudulent charges to their accounts. As long as a card's loss is reported within forty-eight hours its owner is not responsible for any of the charges another person may have rung up on it. Even if a loss is not reported until after forty-eight hours have passed, the cardholder's liability is limited to $50. Cardholders should write down—and carefully save—the toll-free telephone number credit-card issuers provide for reporting missing cards.

If, however, it is a debit card rather than a credit card that has been mislaid, the consequences may be more serious. Debit cards, long popular in Canada and now catching on in the United States as well, are used to deduct money directly from a cardholder's bank account. Unlike an ATM card, which it otherwise resembles, a debit card does not require its owner to punch in a secret personal identification number—a PIN—when using the card to make a purchase. All the debit-card owner has to do is sign a receipt, just as he or she would with a credit card. That means, says Ellen Stark of *Money* magazine, "a debit-card thief may be able to drain your entire checking account simply by faking your signature." When Stark says "drain," she's talking about a sizable cash flow. Debit-card spending limits tend to be high. Bank of America's daily limit on debit-card cash advances and purchases ranges from $700 to $1,200. Chase Manhattan's goes from $1,500 to $5,000. First Union's is $25,000.

Like credit-card customers, owners of debit cards are protected against liability in the event of the loss or theft of a card. But banks are allowed to take up to twenty days to investigate fraud claims and credit a customer's account with money stolen from it. In the meantime the customer could be out a substantial sum. Stolen money will be returned within three weeks to be sure, but until it is, how is the customer going to write out checks or pay bills? In 1998, Visa ordered banks that issue its debit cards to cut the investigation period to just five days. "While five days is sooner than 20, it can be a long time to wait when bills are due," Stark points out.[6] Again, it is likely to seem a longer wait—and a more serious problem—to someone with a low income or shaky credit than to a person with solid financial reserves.

Any credit-card mix-up is going to feel more serious to someone at the bottom of the economic ladder than to someone at or near the top. A man like Thomas Galvin may be taken aback when a valid card is rejected, but he can just reach into his wallet and whip out more plastic. Similarly, if someone like Galvin accidentally misses a payment or is wrongly billed, the fees or temporary expenses he may incur will hardly affect his overall financial situation.

Few of us are in so secure a position. The majority of Americans carry substantial credit-card debt from month to month, and any sudden upset can mean financial chaos. "Sally" was visiting her adult daughter out of state when the younger woman was diagnosed with a life-threatening condition. Throughout January, Sally devoted herself to escorting her daughter to doctors' offices, handling her medical insurance claims, subletting her apartment, arranging storage for her belongings, and all the rest. In February, Sally brought her daughter back home and continued to care for her while resuming her regular job and beginning to catch up on her own affairs. That was when Sally realized that she had missed paying several department-store charge-card bills.

The bills were considerable; they covered Sally's Christmas shopping. Penalty charges cropped up everywhere—$30 here, another $30 there. Interest was mounting. Sally was devastated. Never in great shape, the family's finances now seemed less stable than ever.

That's the sort of thing that can happen, even to a careful and responsible person, which Sally is, when the habit of depending upon credit has left a household financially vulnerable. However, not even the most well-to-do debt-free individual can hope to avoid another kind of trouble associated with credit—the threat of loss of privacy.

Until the credit card was invented, privacy was not much of an issue between borrowers and lenders. People who extended secured loans, such as pawnbrokers and merchants offering installment-plan buying, had little reason to scrutinize a borrower's finances. A pawnbroker could always sell a defaulter's collateral and a storekeeper could repossess an unpaid-for sofa or plow. Neither would be out any money, so neither needed to be too worried about a customer's ability to repay. Revolving credit lenders on the other hand, did have some cause for concern. They were doing business on trust. Still, in earlier times most such lenders—the town doctor, the neighborhood grocer—were personally acquainted with their customers and had a pretty good idea of which ones would meet their obligations and which might not. The universal credit card, which permits perfect strangers to conduct billions of dollars' worth of business with one another in millions of places all over the world, changed all that. As the bankcard fraud cases of the late 1960s demonstrated, it had become essential for someone to do some intensive checking up on the credit worthiness of every single potential cardholder.

"Someone" is really three someones—Equifax Credit Information Services, Experian, and Trans Union Corporation. These are the three largest U.S. credit bureaus, the agencies that banks and other lenders turn to for financial information about would-be borrowers. Each of the three maintains exhaustive records on virtually every American age eighteen and over, all 200 million of them in 1998. And every day the bureaus open thousands of new files as each new wave of America's 70 million under-eighteens approaches adulthood.

What lies tucked away in credit-bureau files? Information about student loans, car payments, home-improvement borrowing, and first, second, and third mortgages. (Most people need to take out a first mortgage to buy a home. Second and third mortgages are generally used to raise money to pay off debts or meet other obligations. The more times a family is forced to mortgage its home, the more precarious its financial situation can be assumed to be). The amount of each loan, the rate at which it is being paid back, late and/or missed payments, delinquencies, bankruptcies—everything finds its way into credit-bureau files.

Credit files also contain information about people's buying habits. This person visits the mall weekly, shopping mainly for clothes. That one orders from catalogs that feature electronic goods. Another spends hundreds on exercise equipment. Based on its spending patterns, this household's annual income is estimated to be about $40,000. Another's is probably closer to $60,000. Equifax, Experian, and Trans Union gather all this information and more, and share it—for a fee—with lenders.[7] Lenders use that information to decide which loan or credit-card applicants are good credit risks and which are not. They also use it to set individual lines of credit and determine how high a rate of interest each particular borrower will be asked to pay. That is why it is so important to maintain a good credit record. People with favorable credit-bureau ratings will have little trouble borrowing when they need to from scrupulous lenders under fair and reasonable conditions. Those with poor ratings may be forced to borrow at exorbitantly high rates from sources that may not even be legal.

THE PRIVACY PROBLEM

From the consumer's point of view, privacy problems arise when a credit bureau shares its information with non-lenders. In the early 1970s, consumer activists charged that one bureau was cooperating with U.S. government investigators looking into suspected tax-fraud cases. All it took was a phone call from someone at the Internal Revenue Service (the IRS is the federal tax-collection agency), and bureau employees would reveal everything they knew or had surmised about a suspect's income and spending habits. Ninety percent of the time, no record was made of such calls. Thus, few of those targeted by the IRS had any way of proving—or even knowing—that their credit privacy was being violated.

Back in the 1970s credit bureaus routinely provided what should have been confidential information to private businesses as well. If the president of a mail-order music club wanted to direct his advertising to people likely to order from his company, for instance, he might ask a credit bureau for the names and addresses of people who had used their credit cards to make music-store purchases. Even in the 1970s, computers were sophisticated enough to enable credit-bureau employees to meet such requests. Businesses of all kinds eagerly bought the specialized mailing lists. In 1974 the U.S. government attempted to put an end to such abuses with a new law, the Federal Privacy Act. Four years later a second federal law was passed to strengthen the provisions of the 1974 measure.[8]

Enacting laws does not guarantee compliance. In 1992 the U.S. government accused Trans Union of selling consumer information to catalog companies, newspaper and magazine subscription salespeople, banks, and insurance companies. Trans Union denied any wrongdoing and the case dragged on until 1998. That year a federal judge found that Trans Union had indeed violated the law and ordered the agency to put an end to its illegal practices. Trans Union executives announced that they would contest the judge's decision—and go right on selling information about the private lives of most of the country's adults and a great many of its teenagers.[9]

Alarming as that sounds, it is even more alarming to realize that credit-bureau information is not limited to facts and figures about car and education loans, estimated incomes, and overdue bills. We use our credit cards to subscribe to magazines as diverse as *Newsweek*, *People*, and *Penthouse*. We use them to contribute to political parties from the mainstream Democrats and Republicans to far-out groups at both ends of the political spectrum. We use credit cards to make charitable and religious donations and to provide financial support to the entire gamut of social causes. Our credit histories may reveal whether we are antiabortion or pro-choice, in favor of gun control or opposed to it, support the notion of white supremacy or find the very idea revolting, and much, much more.

How safe can any of us feel, knowing that kind of personal information is on file—and perhaps for sale?

THE EASIEST TROUBLE

Easy as it is to stumble into credit trouble through no fault of one's own, trouble comes even more easily to those who do make mistakes. For some, the mistake is as simple as giving out a credit-card number on the telephone or over the Internet.

Of course, people sometimes do have occasion to give out their numbers. Anyone who places a telephone call or goes online to order goods or services may want to charge the purchase on a credit card. In that case—when the cardholder himself or herself has initiated the contact—it is generally safe to reveal a card's number.

But a person on the receiving end of a call or Internet communication needs to exercise extreme caution. Never give out a credit-card number when someone phones to say, for example, that you've won a prize but that the caller needs credit-card information in order to verify your identity. The caller may be in the "business" of credit-card theft. Never give out a number over the Internet either, unless the closed-padlock icon appears in the lower left corner of the computer screen. The icon indicates a secure site, one from which a credit-card number cannot be stolen. Remember that although the liability limit on stolen credit cards is low, the inconvenience of coping with the aftermath of credit-card theft can be considerable.

Another opportunity for trouble presents itself when the use of credit collides with another sort of problem—a gambling habit, for instance.

Gambling is increasingly common in the United States. Casinos are legal in twenty-six of the fifty states and lotteries are permitted in thirty-eight. Although state laws set the minimum age for gambling at eighteen or twenty-one, younger teens have little trouble slipping into casinos or laying their hands on lottery tickets. Michael, speaking to a reporter on the understanding that his last name not be used, recalls being just fifteen years old when he began using fake identification to get into casinos in the gambling mecca of Atlantic City, New Jersey. Michael quickly became hooked on gambling. He was addicted to the activity, much as another person might become addicted to tobacco, alcohol, or cocaine. Before long he was betting up to $2,000 a hand at the blackjack table—and stealing from his family to finance his habit.

"By the time I was seventeen," Michael says, "my parents had put a lock on everything in the house—bedrooms, pantries, closets." That was because he was stealing bath towels and selling them at thirty cents apiece for gambling money. Over the next ten years Michael went to prison twice for crimes that included credit-card fraud. Today he is in a treatment program, struggling to put gambling and credit-card crime behind him.[10] Credit troubles are frequently linked to other forms of addiction as well.

The majority of those who find themselves in credit difficulties, however, get there through mistakes that involve carelessness or ignorance. We've already met several young people who fall into this category.

One was Jennifer Dahlin. As we saw in the first chapter, Jennifer made a long string of mistakes. She committed fraud by signing a credit-card application intended for someone else. Only sixteen years old, she did not realize that even if the application had been meant for her she would have needed an adult cosigner. Once Jennifer did receive a card she used it recklessly, squandering money on items of no lasting value, quickly exhausting the card's credit limit, and tumbling deep into debt. "My biggest mistake," Jennifer calls that episode.

Big, but understandable. Jennifer, growing up in poverty, had little experience handling money or credit. Her naïveté nearly landed her in prison. Yet more sophisticated people also make terrible mistakes. Amy Maxwell, the American University student, ran up $17,000 in debts in her freshman year, maxing out all three of her Visa cards. And what about Mark Nyman and Elizabeth Genel? Both had law degrees, yet neither hesitated to plunge a one-income household into nearly half-a-million dollars' worth of debt. Hal McCabe graduated from college owing $80,000, paid it back, then turned around and borrowed $32,000 more. Why are so many people getting into so much trouble?

The answer has several parts. First of all, many Americans, especially those who may be financially unsophisticated, do not fully understand what credit cards are and—more to the point— what they are not.

What credit cards are not is money. From the consumer's point of view they do not even represent money. Signing a credit-card slip is not the same as paying for something with cash or a debit card or a check drawn on funds in an existing banking account. Sure, those doing the signing get to eat the meal, slip on the jacket, play the video game. But unless they can pay their credit-card bills in full as each comes due, their most lasting purchases may turn out to be the debts they have assumed.

Along with debts come interest charges and the possibility of late-payment fees or other penalties. That's another aspect of credit-card use that cardholders tend to overlook—and another part of the reason so many get into trouble. We saw in Chapter Four that even a businessman like Art Goldstein is not immune to treating his credit cards in a most unbusinesslike way. Goldstein must keep a sharp eye on his own business—otherwise why is it successful?—but when it came to his credit card, he let his guard down completely, not even bothering to note the rate of interest he was being charged. Millions of other Americans are equally cavalier. Few take the time to sit back, study the fine print, and accurately calculate credit's ultimate costs.

A third part of the answer as to why some credit-card users run into trouble can be summed up in the word "consumerism." Americans may be the world's most eager consumers. The nation's malls and shopping centers are crowded with stores crammed full of thousands upon thousands of tempting goods and offering hundreds of attractive services. It's hard not to want them all—from that new snowboard to a state-of-the-art computer, from fast-food lunches to portable CD players, from the latest in body piercing to the hottest tape cassette. Can't afford everything? Pull out the plastic. "You can't max out your life if you don't max out your card sometimes," argues Hal McCabe. If the result is going repeatedly into debt, so be it. For some people, constant credit-card overspending can turn into a kind of addiction in itself.

But a person does not have to be addicted to buying on credit to think the way Hal McCabe does. *Buy now, pay later* has been part of the American lifestyle for a long time. In the past, though, local revolving credit borrowing and secured installment-buying plans worked to ensure that most people did not outspend their means. Debts were generally honored.

It's different today. Maxing out has become a way of life for many. So have its consequences—mounting debt, lousy credit ratings, and a surge in bankruptcies and delinquencies.

When Amy Maxwell found herself $17,000 in debt, she took a number of actions. She dropped out of American University and signed up at a community college where she could live and study more cheaply. She took a job and began lobbying for state laws that would limit the amount of credit extended to young people. And she declared personal bankruptcy.

In the past, bankruptcy was a rare disgrace. Even during the Great Depression, fear of being labeled bankrupt led millions to do whatever it took to pay off their debts—sell the house, order the kids to drop out of college, take any menial job just to be earning something—no sacrifice was too great. Since then, attitudes have changed. Bankruptcy has lost much of its stigma, and the number of Americans filing for it increased steadily throughout the 1990s. According to one U.S. lawmaker, more Americans file for bankruptcy each year than graduate from college. In most instances declaring bankruptcy means wiping out credit-card debt and starting over with a clean slate and no feeling of shame.[11]

However, just because bankruptcy is no longer the humiliation it used to be doesn't mean it is without its consequences.

"You'll live with it as a black mark on your credit report for a decade to come," cautions Kerry Hannon in the magazine *U.S. News & World Report*.[12] And that report is the basis upon which lenders decide whether or not a person gets a loan and how much he or she will have to pay for it.

A credit report may also help determine whether a householder or car owner will be able to buy insurance, says Jean Sherman Chatzky of *Money* magazine. "More than 300 auto and home insurers are now consulting credit information when screening applicants," she wrote in 1998. "Folks with a blemish or two on their reports . . . may be denied coverage or shunted to a . . . carrier with higher rates, sometimes 50% to 100% higher than what someone with a clean credit history would get."[13]

How does this apply to an Amy Maxwell? Amy's bankruptcy showed up on her credit report when she was just nineteen years old. Until she is twenty-nine at the very least, that information will stay in credit-bureau files, possibly keeping her from being able to borrow to buy a house or a car. Even if she is somehow able to purchase either, obtaining insurance may be impossible or extremely expensive. Nor does Amy's bankruptcy filing eliminate all her debts. She will have to pay back any student loans and back taxes she owes. Parents of young children who file for bankruptcy are also obliged to keep up court-ordered child-support payments.

The consequences of bankruptcy may be more serious in the future. Congress may enact a law that would force those filing for bankruptcy to repay much of their credit-card debt.

Even those who stay out of bankruptcy court face a long, tough struggle when credit-card excesses have left them in a hole. Mark Nyman and Elizabeth Genel will probably emerge from debt eventually, but their badly flawed credit histories will continue to haunt them. Information about overdue bills and missed payments stays on the record for seven years, according to Kerry Hannon. Already into their thirties when they fully understood the trouble they had brought upon themselves in their teens and twenties, the couple know they may be middle-aged or older before their troubles are at last behind them.

Where do people with poor credit histories or those who have filed for bankruptcy turn when they absolutely have to borrow? To so-called subprime lenders.

SUBPRIME LENDING

"Prime" means first in excellence, quality, or value. Subprime means anything less. "On a scale where A is the best credit rating," says *Consumer Reports* magazine, "'subprime' refers to borrowers with a rating of B, C, or D."[14] One leading U.S. subprime credit-card issuer is Delaware's Cross Country Bank.

As we saw in Chapter Four, Cross Country charges its Visa customers a $100 approval fee in addition to a $50 annual fee. Since subprime lenders strictly limit the amount of credit they extend, that can mean a $150 charge for a line of credit that may come to no more than $350. A hundred and fifty dollars plus interest—that's a lot to pay to borrow $350. But credit-card applicants whose ratings do not qualify them for other banks' cards have little choice but to accept deals like Cross Country's.

"I'm trying to rebuild my credit," one Cross Country customer who describes his rating as "not up to power" told *Consumer Reports.* "When you find someone who offers you a chance to do that, you grab it."

Grabbing it turned out to be even more expensive than this man anticipated. He claims that Cross Country charged him $200 in overlimit fees even though he never exceeded his line of credit. According to him, the bank also imposed $25 late fees on payments made well before their due date. Cross Country even charged the man $1.50 per call when he telephoned to question the penalties! Cross Country officials deny the man's allegations, but admit that 50 percent of the bank's credit-card income comes from fees. On average, U.S. banks make only 9.1 percent of their credit-card income from fees. Cross Country "is a very expensive bank for borrowers," concludes Warren Heller, research director of a Massachusetts bank-rating firm.[15] But more than 1.7 million subprime credit-card owners were stuck doing business with it in 1998.

Other subprime lenders are to be found in the home-equity loan industry. As mentioned earlier, home-equity loans allow people to borrow money using their homes as collateral. Unlike a first home mortgage that provides a home buyer with money to make a down payment and begin purchasing a house, home-equity loans permit people to borrow against a house they already own or are in the process of buying through a separate mortgage. People may use the money from a home-equity loan to fix up a house in need of repairs, rid themselves of longstanding education or credit-card debts, pay off bank or auto loans, or meet other obligations.

One selling point for home-equity loans is their convenience. Home-equity borrowers replace a confusing number of different payments to a variety of individual creditors with a single monthly payment to the home-equity company. Another advantage of this type of loan is that home-equity interest rates may be significantly lower than credit-card interest rates. As long as the amount of a home-equity loan is geared to a borrower's income and his or her ability to repay it promptly, such a loan can be a useful financial tool.

Home-equity lenders who fall into the subprime category, however, may not take care to base their loans on a borrower's ability to repay. Their loans are more likely to be based upon the value of the borrower's home. Fred Wood of Atlanta, Georgia, was unlucky enough to run into such a home-equity lender.

Wood, age fifty-eight, dropped out of school when he was in the eighth grade. A part-time fast-food worker, he wasn't earning much of a salary. He did own his own home, though, a house worth about $40,000 left to him by his father. Based upon that asset, a subprime home-equity lender offered Wood a $39,000 loan. Wood took up the offer.

Of course, there was no way he could repay such an amount. Even with three quarters of his salary going to the home-equity company, Wood fell further and further behind on his payments. "Lots of nights I'd wake up and sit on the edge of the bed worrying," he says. He knows there is a good chance the home-equity company will foreclose on his house, taking possession of it in order to sell it and make good the loan. In the prime lending market a person's home is ordinarily protected from foreclosure, even in the event of a bankruptcy filing. But Wood is not dealing with a prime lender. If he loses his home he will have nothing left.

Closely related to subprime home-equity loans are subprime home-improvement loans. Mary and Wilton Burton are in their eighties and live near Boston, Massachusetts. In 1995 a subprime lender approached them with a loan offer. (Subprime lenders target potential customers and pursue them with attractive-sounding proposals just as avidly as credit-card issuers do.)

The Burtons accepted the offer, figuring on spending $2,000 to repair their leaky roof. The man who arranged the loan "didn't ask me how much my income was," Wilton Burton points out. In fact, it was just $10,200 annually. Yet the loan agreement the couple signed called for monthly payments of $708—a total of $8,496 a year. Unable to make their scheduled payments, the Burtons took out a second loan. By now their debt was up to $83,000—and the loan company was threatening to foreclose on the house they had called their own for twenty-five years. "We're living on the edge," Burton says. "We don't know if we have a home or we don't."

People like the Burtons and Fred Wood may face uncertain futures, but for their subprime creditors the outlook is bright. U.S. government figures show that subprime lending has become a $125 billion-a-year industry.[16] And whereas subprime lending used to be the business of small fly-by-night companies, that is no longer the case. Some of the nation's largest financial institutions are now getting into the act. "Big lenders like Chase Manhattan, Norwest, Nationsbank, General Electric, Keycorp, Countrywide Credit Industries and others are expanding their lending to 'subprime' borrowers," says one financial writer.[17] The Burtons' first loan came from a financial subsidiary of the Ford Motor Company. Executives at corporations like Ford and Chase Manhattan recognize a financial bonanza when they see one. "The potential in subprime lending has never been more clear," is the upbeat message caroled in one industry pamphlet, "partly because there haven't been so many subprime Americans since the Great Depression."

Every year approximately three million of those "subprime" Americans find themselves caught up in rent-to-own schemes. Rent to own is nothing new, although the industry's soaring profit levels were making headlines as the year 2000 began. At that point, the nation's 7,500-odd rent-to-own stores were raking in $4 billion a year.

For low-income customers, the attraction of rent-to-own is that it allows them to buy, bit by bit, items they would not otherwise be able to afford. Rent to own enables even those without credit cards to buy on credit. Its disadvantage is its expense. As we saw in Chapter Three, the final cost of a rent-to-own household appliance or a piece of furniture can be more than double what its price would be in a retail store. A rent-to-own customer who pays $200 over the course of a year for an item that goes for $100 retail is in effect paying interest at a rate of 100 percent annually. Since a number of states do not allow such high interest rates, rent-to-own operators describe their charges as "fees."

Fourteen-year-old Stefan Jones knows firsthand what it can be like to deal with a rent-to-own company. Stefan's mother, Cherese Lindsey, had fallen behind in making payments on a rent-to-own sofa and love seat she was trying to buy from a Curtis Mathes store in Minnesota. The teenager was alone in the pair's apartment when Curtis Mathes collectors showed up to repossess the furniture. Stefan refused to unlock the door and eventually, shouting and cursing, the collectors left.

One day soon after that Stefan and his mother came home to an empty—a very empty—apartment. The door had been kicked in. Sofa and love seat gone—along with the television, VCR, and microwave that Lindsey had bought and long since finished paying for. "I just started crying," she mourned.

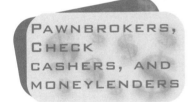

PAWNBROKERS, CHECK CASHERS, AND MONEYLENDERS

Other sources of subprime loans include pawnbrokers, check cashers, and moneylenders. All are apt to charge exorbitantly for their services, either taking advantage of lax state anti-usury laws or getting around such laws by calling their charges fees. Pawnbrokers, for example, were imposing effective interest rates of up to 240 percent in 1998.[18]

As ancient a trade as pawnbrokering is, new twists on the business are always emerging. One recent innovation is car-title pawn or car-title lending.

Under a car-title pawn agreement a car owner hands over the title, or ownership, of his or her vehicle in return for a cash loan. The borrower also retains the right to continue using the car—unless he or she defaults on a payment. Defaulting is likely, given car-title pawn's steep monthly repayment rates. In Georgia it is legal for car-title lenders to charge interest rates of 25 percent a month. That's 300 percent a year—three times the amount of the loan. In 1994, Florida lawmakers "limited" the yearly interest rate on car-title loans in that state to "only" 264 percent. Car-title lending, like the subprime home-equity loan business, used to be the province of small companies. Again like the home-equity loan business, car-title pawn is now going big time. One industry leader, Georgia's Title Loans of America, is financed in part by a subsidiary of the huge Fleet Financial Group.

Another newcomer to the subprime credit market is the payday loan company. Payday lenders agree to advance a sum of money—$100, say—to someone desperate for a relatively small amount of cash. In exchange for the $100, the borrower gives the loan company a check for $130. Company officials agree not to cash the check until the borrower's next weekly payday when, presumably, he or she will have enough money in the bank to cover it. When payday does come, however, the borrower may still be in a hole financially and unable to afford repayment. In that case his only option may be to renew the $100 loan for another week—and for another $30 fee. A person who renews a $100 loan in this way for a year will have paid an APR of 780 percent. In 1992 there were three hundred payday loan companies operating in the United States. Seven years later there were 8,000. As of mid-1999, such businesses were legal in thirty-one states.[19]

Check-cashing stores are also part of the sleazier side of the subprime lending market. People who cannot afford the expense of maintaining checking accounts of their own use such stores to cash checks when they need to. Check cashers offer other services as well. For a fee they will draw up checks for their customers to use to pay rent, utility, and cable-TV bills as well as parking tickets. Some issue money orders. Check cashers' charges are steep, but that doesn't stop over ten million Americans—most of them desperately needy, with poor credit ratings that shut them off from more conventional financial institutions—from turning to them on a regular basis.[20]

Finally, skirting the very fringes of legality, not infrequently slipping over the edge, are moneylenders. The dictionary defines moneylender simply as "one whose business is lending money at an interest rate," but the popular imagination invests the word with more sinister connotations. *Moneylender* evokes images of shady dealings, dark alleys, sky-high payments, loan sharks, threats of violence, even organized crime. That may be why we are saddened, but perhaps not too surprised, to come across news stories like this one:

Lee Kyung Bok owned a grocery store in a Korean-American neighborhood in the New York City borough of Queens. The store was called Sunny Supermarket—an irony, considering Bok's bleak financial position. Cash was short, then shorter still, and Bok appealed to a well-known local moneylender for help. The moneylender agreed to a $10,000 loan, with interest payments of $125 a week.

Bok struggled to make the payments, but in vain. He arranged to meet with the moneylender and his wife. To beg for more money? Plead for time to repay? Argue about the terms of the loan?

No one can be sure. All that is certain is that a gun was present. The moneylender and his wife were found shot dead. Bok was arrested on murder charges.[21]

So violent an ending to a story of borrowing and debt is rare. But the feelings that led up to that ending are not rare in the least. The mounting desperation as debt grows, the knowledge that it is becoming more and more unmanageable, that there may be no way out, these feelings are all too common among people today. Jennifer Dahlin must have experienced such feelings. So must Mark Nyman and Elizabeth Genel. So must Amy Maxwell.

Amy has experienced another feeling as well—the feeling that she was victimized by the credit industry. Now she is fighting back.

SIX
CONSUMER PROTECTION

"I truly believe I am a victim of credit-card companies," Amy Maxwell says today. That conviction led Amy, then a community-college student, to undertake a letter-writing campaign, hoping to persuade legislators in her home state of New York to pass laws that would keep other young people from getting into the kind of credit trouble she did.

CREDIT ON CAMPUS

What sorts of laws? One New York proposal would make it illegal for credit-card issuers to solicit students on the campuses of state-run colleges and universities.

Roger Witherspoon supports the proposal. Witherspoon is vice president for student development at John Jay College of Criminal Justice, part of the New York state university system. He has prohibited anyone from handing out credit-card applications on the John Jay campus and would like to see the ban extended to cover every one of the state's public institutions of higher education. Lawmakers in Massachusetts and Kansas have considered similar bills. "Kids are dropping out of school, and their credit is ruined for life," Witherspoon asserts. The best way to protect young people, he believes, is to keep credit-card vendors away from them.[1]

Others beg to differ. The vendors themselves certainly do not like the idea. Even some of the consumer advocates who are most concerned about the misuse of credit by young cardholders have their doubts about proposals like the one Witherspoon endorses. They point out that barring credit-card solicitations at state colleges would have done nothing to protect Amy Maxwell at American University. American University is a private college, not a public one. No state legislature has the right to tell private-school officials whom they may or may not welcome on campus. Besides, college students are hardly confined to campus. They may run into credit-card marketers in stores and banks. They may see them handing out applications on street corners or in bus stations. Who is going to "protect" them then? Are college officials going to search student mailboxes for credit-card applications? Monitor Internet application sites? A better way to keep students from misusing credit, many say, is to set strict limits on the amount of credit each is offered.

That's how two Canadian girls found their mother handling the credit-card question when they went off to college. "I got each of them a Visa," the mother explains, describing the cards as "specifically student," with credit limits of $500. A student MasterCard sold out of Las Vegas, Nevada, caps credit at just $100. How about writing similar limits into state laws?

Many think it's a good idea. Offering a college freshman $17,000 worth of credit is unconscionable, they contend. And what about card issuers' habit of encouraging students to include their education loans as personal income? Loans are not income; they are debt. Inflating lines of credit by counting as assets parental allowances and credit available on other cards should not be permissible either, critics say.

Others are not so sure about arbitrary limits. One reason many high-school and college students give for wanting credit cards is that using one allows them to start building credit histories. Graduating with solid credit ratings will make it easier and cheaper for them to borrow once they're on their own. How can they build good records if they're kept from borrowing freely and proving they can be trusted to pay back the money? Even if limits are generous—$2,000, instead of $100 or $500—many young people would still object to being penalized just because of their age. In fact, most youthful credit-card owners do act responsibly. A 1998 survey showed that 59 percent of college students say they pay their monthly balances in full and on time. Eighty-two percent claim to maintain balances of $1,000 or less.[2]

Credit-card issuers are no more enthusiastic about severely low credit limits than they are about the idea of being barred from public-college campuses. They don't like another suggestion—requiring people under age eighteen or still financially dependent upon their families to receive formal parental permission to own a credit card—any better. Roger Witherspoon thinks he knows why. "Credit-card companies have saturated the market," he says, "and college kids are the only market left." Card issuers are not going to look favorably on any proposal that threatens to cut them off from that market.

Card issuers have never been enthusiastic about the idea of legal curbs on their activities. In the beginning few saw the need for any regulation at all. It took a near disaster to convince industry leaders that some rules might not be a bad idea after all.

REGULATING AN INDUSTRY

By the late 1960s, BankAmericard (now Visa) and Interbank (Master Charge and later, MasterCard) were engaged in a battle for domination of the bankcard market. Determined to win over consumers still reluctant to apply for credit cards that were accepted by only a limited number of businesses, the rival companies launched drives to get their cards into the hands of every American possible. Millions of unsolicited BankAmericards and Master Charge cards were mailed out. The cards, fully activated and ready to use, began turning up at addresses around the country. Each was stamped with a valid account number and the name of its intended owner.

Many of the cards reached the people whose names appeared on them. Others arrived at addresses from which people had long since moved away. Some had gone out to people who were no longer living. Quite a few went to children, including newborns. A surprising number proved to have been sent to the family pet.

The real problem, though, was that many of the misdirected cards were kept by those who happened to receive them and used to run up fraudulent charges. For the industry, that meant huge losses—$115.5 million in 1970 alone.

For the people whose names appeared on the stolen cards, the situation was nightmarish. Many had never used a credit card—never even wanted one—yet here they were, thousands of dollars in "debt." When they complained to BankAmericard and Master Charge, their protests were brushed aside. Both companies showed what Lewis Mandell calls an "unwillingness and/or inability . . . to protect their customers." Both called in collection agencies. Both threatened to garnishee wages and seize personal property if "debts" were not paid. *Innocent until proven guilty* may be a basic assumption of U.S. law, but to the bankcard issuers of the late 1960s it was more like *guilty unless you can prove yourself innocent.* It was up to the victims of the fraud—and of the mailings that had led to it—to retrieve their financial reputations. Often that meant hiring a high-priced attorney and appearing in a court of law.

Finally, in May 1970, the Federal Trade Commission (FTC) acted on behalf of beleaguered consumers. The FTC is the government agency assigned to protect Americans from unfair business practices. FTC officials ordered an immediate, temporary end to the mailing of unsolicited credit cards. President Richard M. Nixon later made the ban permanent.

"The ban on unsolicited cards probably came at an opportune time for the bankcard companies," Mandell says in retrospect. It put an end to much of the fraud, saving the industry millions. It also gave companies time to reorganize their operations and get them running more smoothly before resuming the effort to expand their cardholder bases. Moreover, by the time the ban went into effect the mass mailings had had the desired effect. Millions of Americans had started using the cards they'd received. BankAmericard and Master Charge had as many new customers as each could handle. In 1974 the bankcard industry enjoyed the most profitable year it had yet seen.

GOVERNING GROWTH

As the industry grew so did public awareness that still more regulation was necessary. Cardholders needed assurances that issuers would pay serious attention to complaints about billing errors, for example. No one wanted to repeat the experience of those mistakenly billed in the wake of the ill-thought-out mass mailings of the 1960s. Consumers also needed a better understanding of how much their credit cards were going to cost them in the long run. Information about annual percentage rates, grace periods, and other technicalities often lay buried in a maze of legal and mathematical mumbo jumbo. Card issuers had to be compelled to spell out such information in plain and simple language.

Other issues cropped up. People learned that credit bureaus were cooperating with federal tax fraud investigators and selling personal information to businesses. Such practices indicated a need for laws to protect consumers against invasions of their privacy. At the same time, individual consumers had to be guaranteed the right to examine their own credit records whenever they suspected that errors might have crept into them. When consumers did find errors—a not uncommon occurrence—they needed legal assurances that corrections would be made promptly.

Another unresolved matter involved access to credit. In the 1960s and throughout much of the 1970s, lenders routinely made decisions about extending credit based on such characteristics as race or gender. A single woman—even one earning a good income—would be turned down for a home mortgage, for instance, whereas a single man with the same income would not. A man whose address placed him in a largely black inner-city neighborhood might be denied credit, while a man with similar assets living in a well-to-do suburb would get it. As the law stood, it was legal to discriminate in such a fashion.

One by one, Congress addressed consumer concerns. In 1972 it passed the Fair Credit Billing Act. That law forced card issuers to acknowledge complaints about billing errors and set time limits for them to conduct formal investigations and make corrections or offer explanations. That law was updated in 1975. The Federal Privacy Act became law in 1974 and its provisions were strengthened four years later. The Equal Credit Opportunity Act that took effect in 1977 made it illegal to deny credit based on sex, race, national origin, or marital status.[3] Another law made it mandatory for credit-card issuers to display information regarding their "terms and conditions"—APR, grace period, annual fee, transaction fees, and method of computing interest—clearly and prominently on application forms.

Congress continues to refine credit rules and regulations. In 1997 federal law was changed to make it easier for consumers to fix mistakes in their credit records. "Banks, department stores and other companies are now legally responsible for the accuracy of the information they provide to credit bureaus," says *Money* magazine. That takes the burden of proving that an error has been made off the consumer and puts it where it belongs, on whomever has provided the misinformation. In another change for the better, consumers are now entitled to a free look at their credit files whenever they have been turned down for any one of a wide range of benefits, from opening a cell phone account to renting an apartment. Until the new law took effect, free access came only after a person was turned down for a loan or credit card.[4]

CONSUMERS AT RISK

Not all rules and regulations are so consumer friendly, however. The Florida and Georgia laws that allow car-title pawn companies to charge interest at rates of 264 and 300 percent a year respectively are examples of laws that are downright consumer hostile. *Consumer Reports* tells us that after the Florida legislature passed its car-title pawn law in 1995, the legislature's own experts urged its repeal. Lawmakers rejected the idea two years in a row. During those two years, the car-title pawn industry contributed over $94,000 to Florida legislators of both political parties.

Other state laws, although less blatantly skewed against borrowers, nevertheless offer little real protection. As reported by *The World Almanac*, twenty-six states placed no limits on credit-card interest rates in 1998. Many that did set limits had high ones: 24 percent in Maryland; 30 percent in New Jersey; 36 percent for amounts up to $1,000 in Wyoming.

States may also set maximum allowable interest rates on non-credit-card loans. In twelve states that maximum is described as "any agreed rate" or "no limit." In Louisiana it is 36 percent a year for loans of up to $1,400; in Florida it's 30 percent a year for loans of up to $2,000.

Other laws that leave borrowers vulnerable include those that allow such subprime lenders as rent-to-own operators to describe their charges as fees in order to get around interest limits that do exist. Forty-five states had such laws in 1998. Even that wasn't enough to satisfy the rent-to-own industry, which was trying to get Congress to make it illegal to regulate their transactions as credit, retail, or installment sales in any state.[5] Consumer advocates denounced the industry's effort. It's good that society has abandoned the old way of thinking that equated the taking of interest with usury and condemned both, they say. But laws that allow lenders to squeeze profits from the poorest at interest rates of 200 or 300 percent a year go too far in the other direction.

For all the state and federal credit-related laws already on the books, most consumer advocates say more are needed. For starters, they would like to see states tighten laws governing subprime lending.

All subprime borrowers share one characteristic: They are imperfect credit risks. A large percentage of them have a couple of other things in common as well: They are middle-aged or older and members of racial or ethnic minorities.

"We have financial apartheid in our country," says William Brennan, an Atlanta, Georgia, lawyer. "Apartheid" refers to a system of strict racial separation. Many of Brennan's clients have fallen victim to abusive home-equity loan schemes. A disproportionate number of them are elderly and black. More needs to be done to protect such people, Brennan and others believe. Society has rethought its attitudes toward the ethics of borrowing and lending in the past, they say. Now it is time to do so again. Perhaps Congress could make more low-interest home-improvement loans available to subprime credit risks. It could pass laws making it harder for lenders to target people like Fred Wood and Mary and Wilton Burton, maneuver them into crushing debt, and threaten foreclosure.

Other critics of subprime lending laws and practices voice a different type of concern. "Risk warfare" is the phrase banking consultant Edward Furash uses to describe the fast-growing subprime lending market. "There is an expansion of credit across the board for people who wouldn't have gotten credit" in the past, he says. "And it's making me nervous." The U.S. economy was strong in the late 1990s, Furash points out. It won't always be. Good economic times are invariably followed by bad. When the economy does turn sour, thousands upon thousands of subprime borrowers already struggling to make ends meet are sure to fall into delinquency or bankruptcy. With some of the nation's largest banks now in the subprime lending business, those delinquencies and bankruptcies could send shock waves through the entire banking industry, not just one obscure portion of it.[6] Bad times could turn into outright depression, which is why many financial analysts are calling for tightening rules aimed at tying loans to a borrower's income and ability to repay.

We saw earlier in this chapter that lawmakers in a few states have debated regulating credit-card solicitations on some college campuses. The idea of imposing credit limits on young people is also under consideration. But what about credit limits for older people?

In 1993 credit cards issued in the United States carried an average $2,500 line of credit. By 1997 the average credit limit had climbed to $3,500, a 40 percent increase. Of course most people do not use all the credit available to them. Credit-card convenience users hardly draw upon their credit at all.

Even so, card issuers keep upping the amounts they are willing to lend. In 1990 lenders were offering Americans roughly twice as much credit as they were using. By 1996 they were offering them 3.4 times as much. In March 1998 lines of credit on American credit cards amounted to 4.2 times the amount cardholders were actually borrowing.

Why the generosity? Credit-card issuers want to make it as easy as possible for consumers to borrow—and have to repay with interest—more and more and more. To them, that apparently makes good business sense.

For consumers, soaring lines of credit make very little sense. What if a cardholder faces sudden illness or the unexpected loss of a job? In an emergency, a person may well succumb to the temptation to borrow up to his or her credit limit, however unrealistically high that limit may be. And don't forget that the average U.S. cardholding household has eleven different cards, each with its own separate line of credit. Maxing out on all of them could leave a family owing many times what it can afford to pay back.

Another problem with very high lines of credit, experts say, is that they can stand in the way of a consumer's ability to get other types of loans. Home-mortgage providers, for example, may refuse to lend to a cardholder who has what appears to be an excessive amount of credit, even when that credit isn't being used. That is because mortgage lenders fear that if the credit is ever used, the cardholder will fall into unmanageable debt and default on all loans including any mortgage loan.[7] So, odd as it may seem, consumers who insist upon lower lines of credit on their cards may actually find it easier, not harder, to borrow when they really need to. If the industry as a whole adopted—or was legally forced to adopt—a policy of limiting credit for cardholders of all ages, there would be the added advantage of limiting it for young people without discriminating against them on the basis of age.

PRIVACY REVISITED

Finally there is the matter of privacy. Privacy rules have applied to the credit-card industry for over a quarter of a century, but now, with the increasing popularity of the Internet and Internet shopping and banking, those rules may need revising. Figures show that the incidence of Internet shopping rose sharply in 1998. By early the next year 3.7 million people had applied for credit cards online.[8] It was expected that $40.5 billion would have been borrowed over the Internet by 2001.[9]

Surveys indicate that privacy is the number-one concern among people who buy, bank, and borrow online. According to one FTC study, 87 percent of Internet retail sites collect personal data from those who visit them, yet only 13 percent warn visitors that they are doing so. Of the thousands of Web sites designed specifically for children, 89 percent ask for personal information. Some questions are meant to solicit facts about money gifts a child may have received, or about bank accounts in his or her name. Fewer than 10 percent of children's Web sites give parents the opportunity to examine, correct, or remove the information provided. Just 2 percent of Internet retailers had drawn up detailed plans aimed at protecting consumer privacy in 1998.[10] Much of the information collected is routine—names, addresses, credit-card numbers. But the often-asked questions about age, sex, occupation, hobbies, and finances have nothing to do with making purchases and are no doubt enabling retailers to assemble detailed mailing lists that they will either use themselves or sell to other businesses.

Internet retailers don't even have to ask questions to learn a certain amount about their customers. "The very kinds of sites we visit reveal a great deal about us to those who want our money," Rob Fixmer writes in *The New York Times*. "When we buy products or enter contests or register to use a site, we reveal not only who we are but a great deal about how we live."[11]

Some Internet merchandisers ask visitors to reveal even more, going so far as to ask visitors for information that's not theirs to give. Facts about parents or other family members should never be shared over the Internet. Nor is it ever okay to reveal a parent's credit-card number without getting permission first—something else Internet retailers may neglect to tell their underage visitors. One San Antonio, Texas, teacher reports that it's not uncommon for her fifth-grade students to "go get into Mom's and Dad's purse and get a credit card."[12] Even very young children have been known to use the cards to go Internet shopping—and spend large amounts of money. It is true that parents may be able to return merchandise and have their accounts credited with the amount spent. Still, straightening matters out can be a tedious process. Using a parent's credit card without permission constitutes a kind of in-family fraud, or at the very least, a lack of communication and understanding regarding family finances.

Another factor adding urgency to the call for stricter privacy rules is the phenomenon known as "identity theft." Identity thieves gather information about a person: name, address, Social Security number, credit-card numbers. Some manage to obtain valid photo IDs and such unique identifying details as a mother's maiden name. Thieves use the information to open fake credit accounts, engage in tax fraud and the like. It can take years for a victim of identity theft to win back his or her good name.

New technologies are changing the Internet almost daily—another reason many see for new privacy laws. A computer chip introduced early in 1999 is capable of "reading" a person's fingerprints. Expected to be built into notebook and desktop computers, bankcards, cell phones, door and car locks, drivers' licenses, and various other objects, the chip will identify users and allow them—and only them—access to their property, including credit. Some hail the chip as a way of protecting property from computer intruders. Others fear it will only make it easier for Internet retailers to "spy" on their customers, collecting spending information and pitching products accordingly. Banks, insurance companies, magazine publishers, and other businesses that want to "track our every move, profile our every passion, anticipate our every need," may be able to use the chip to do all that and more, Rob Fixmer warns. A few people wonder whether the IRS or other government agencies will also see the chip as an investigatory tool.[13]

If so-called smart cards catch on they, too, seem sure to demand new rules to govern their use. Smart cards are embedded with sophisticated computer chips. A user inserts a card into an ATM and instructs the machine to transfer a certain cash value to it. Then he or she uses the card to make purchases in stores, buy items from vending machines, pay bus fares, and so forth. The cost of each purchase is automatically deducted from the card's cash value. When the card's money supply is exhausted, its owner simply stops by an ATM and replenishes it. Early in 1998 many were predicting that smart cards would transform the economy by replacing cash altogether and turning our familiar coins and paper money into things of the past. After a disappointing smart-card test in New York City, however, some changed their minds.[14] Of course the disappointing performance of early bankcards turned out to be no indicator of the credit-card industry's later success.

Aware of public uneasiness with regard to novelties like smart cards and the fingerprint chip and sensitive to other privacy issues as well, the FTC warned Internet sellers that they must come up with self-regulating policies. Unless the industry put strict rules in place—and stuck by them—federal regulators promised to ask Congress for legislation to do it for them.

SELF-REGULATION

Many consumer advocates feel that federal privacy legislation for the Internet will indeed turn out to be necessary. Yet successful self-regulation is not out of the question. Already, the credit industry has taken some steps to look out for consumers and offer help to those in trouble.

The National Foundation for Consumer Credit is the largest and best-known industry consumer-assistance organization. It has 1,450 offices throughout the United States, Puerto Rico, Canada, and Mexico. Many of its credit counseling agencies are known as Consumer Credit Counseling Service (CCCS). The nonprofit agencies have widespread community support. Banks and other lending institutions that prefer that financially troubled consumers pay off their debts instead of declaring bankruptcy contribute to the agencies when a client chooses to adopt a debt repayment plan.

It costs about $9 a month to use Consumer Credit Counseling Service. (Anyone who cannot afford the $9 receives free services.) Counselors help clients organize their finances and figure out debt repayment schedules. They talk with creditors and try to get them to extend payback times, even to reduce interest rates and waive fees. They offer instruction in working out and following monthly budgets.

A warning for anyone in need of a credit-counseling agency comes from *Consumer Reports*: "Don't confuse the credit-counseling centers with companies that claim they can repair your credit," the magazine advises readers. "The latter prey on overextended consumers by charging high fees, supposedly to erase a negative credit record." Only consumers themselves can repair their faulty credit histories. And they can do that only by making regular payments for however long it takes to get back on track financially.[15]

Lenders have developed other consumer-oriented programs. In 1999, Chase Manhattan, the nation's third largest bank, undertook to help provide loans to small businesspeople in the New York City area.

Under this program Chase works with what are called community development financial institutions. The community groups lend to people and businesses that mainstream lenders might regard as subprime business risks: the amateur cook eager to start a professional catering service or the karate buff who hopes to open a school. Loan amounts range from a few thousand dollars to an average of $20,000. Chase Manhattan's part in the venture is determining which loan applicants are good enough credit risks—and have sound enough business plans—to qualify for loans. That's a process that can cost as much as $3,000 per applicant, far too much for a community financial institution to spend. Chase is not offering the actual loans, but it is making them possible.

"This is a first," says Chase executive vice president Carol J. Parry. "We do all the work and the community development financial institutions benefit. I don't know of any other bank that does this."[16]

Maybe others will start. What is more, banks can extend other types of free or low-cost services to borrowers categorized as subprime. At least one New York City bank has agreed to begin offering free checking accounts to people formerly dependent upon the hyper-expensive services of check-cashing outlets.[17] In 1999, however, the U.S. Congress voted against legislation that would have forced banks nationwide to offer low-cost checking accounts to the needy.[18]

Still, lenders claim that they are looking out for consumers. The Sears department store chain has introduced a low-credit-limit charge card for first-time cardholders. Even the biggest credit-card companies are getting into the act. Visa representatives now arrive on college campuses with materials designed to help students plan their financial futures responsibly. MasterCard commercials aired on MTV depict a young credit-card over-spender whose possessions are seen vanishing one by one. Warns a stern voice-over: "If you max out on your credit card and buy things you can't afford, you won't have anything to worry about."

MasterCard maintains that credit-card companies are serious about not letting cardholders, especially young ones, get into trouble. "The industry has a commitment that we educate these young people, so they use their cards wisely," says Charlotte Newton, MasterCard's vice president of consumer affairs.[19]

Maybe so. But where does "education" begin as far as MasterCard is concerned? With seventeen- and eighteen-year-olds learning financial skills on college campuses? With high-school students and their preteen siblings watching warning ads along with their favorite music videos?

Or does the educating start even earlier? Some are convinced it does. Why else, they ask, would the nation's three-year-olds be clamoring for the Barbie that comes with her *very own* *MasterCard*?

SEVEN
CONSUMER EDUCATION

MasterCard and Mattel, the toy company that manufactures the Barbie line of dolls, defend Cool Shoppin' Barbie vigorously. According to them, Barbie is supposed to be seen as a business owner earning money, not as a consumer spending it. They point to the message on the box Barbie comes in: "Be a smart credit card shopper: Set a budget and stick to it." MasterCard points as well to its twenty-four-page booklet aimed at parents, "Kids, Cash, Plastic and You." The booklet is available free to anyone who calls Mattel and asks for it. "A cool educational opportunity," is how Durant Abernethy, president and CEO of the National Foundation for Consumer Credit, describes Cool Shoppin' Barbie.

It certainly is educational, outraged consumer advocates respond. What exactly is it teaching, though? If Barbie is supposed to own a store why do the pictures on the box show her carrying shopping bags, rather than helping customers or arranging merchandise? If this Barbie is selling, why is she called Cool Shoppin' Barbie? The answer is plain. Despite anything MasterCard or Mattel may say, Barbie is buying.

On a deeper level, though, MasterCard and Mattel are right. Barbie is definitely selling.

The most obvious thing she is selling is MasterCard. As credit-card expert Gerri Detweiler says, this toy is a vehicle for introducing MasterCard to some of America's youngest citizens. It is intended to instill brand loyalty that will last a lifetime.

Barbie is selling something else as well—the very concept of credit itself. With this toy, credit is the name of the game. Credit is fun. It gets you cute clothes and a day at the mall. Credit cards are playthings.

What Barbie is not selling—or teaching—is anything about how credit works or how to use it wisely. Sure, there's that message on the box and the offer of an informational booklet. But how many busy parents are going to take the time to phone for a booklet, then sit down and study it with their children? Especially parents who saw no harm in buying this particular doll and allowing their children to treat credit cards as toys in the first place? How many preschoolers, kindergartners, and first and second graders will be able to read the message on the box—much less understand it? How many Barbie fans old enough to read will keep the box and review its message every time they take Barbie "shoppin'"? Nothing directly associated with this toy suggests that credit cards buy debt or that misusing them can get a person into trouble. "If they really want to educate kids, they would include a bill and make them fork over interest payments," Detweiler says tartly.[1]

FINANCIAL LESSONS

A few young Americans are getting such reality-based lessons. Eighth graders at a West Milford, New Jersey, school raised money by selling candy and magazine subscriptions. Then, instead of pooling the money and using it for class trips or projects, school officials set up separate accounts in the name of each participating student. The more money a student had raised, the more went into his or her account. Students will keep the accounts until they graduate, drawing on them to fund extracurricular activities. The school's goal is to turn out savvy consumers who understand the relationship between earning and saving and shopping and paying bills.

Other schools have similar goals. Junior-high students in Casselberry, Florida, were encouraged to learn basic business skills by setting up and running a food concession business. Fourth graders in Haledon, New Jersey, go on practice shopping trips, learning how to get the most for their money. Teachers, principals, and students interested in establishing similar programs can get help from such organizations as the Manhattan-based National Council on Economic Education and the National Endowment for Financial Education of Denver, Colorado. Help comes via the Internet, too. Eastern Michigan University's National Institute for Consumer Education offers consumer-oriented lesson plans that include tips on how young people age eighteen and up can obtain their own credit cards and use them to build positive credit ratings. The lessons further suggest that younger teens may want to apply for a card with a parent or guardian as cosigner. (A list of resources can be found at the end of this book.)

Yet relatively few schools take advantage of such lesson plans. There were 70 million Americans under the age of eighteen in 1998, but the National Council on Economic Education could claim to be reaching only about 7.5 million of them. Just fourteen states have agreed to incorporate formal economics lessons into school curriculums, even on the high school level.[2] Informal lessons, on the other hand, go on nonstop.

THIS SCHOOL BROUGHT TO YOU BY . . .

Step into almost any public school in the country today and you've entered a veritable marketplace. High above the gym floor floats a banner advertising Pepsi. A first-grade teacher hands out free book covers promoting Kellogg's Frosted Flakes and Lay's potato chips. Members of a fourth-grade class will be rewarded with Pizza Hut coupons for every library book they finish reading. In the media room children watch a movie about dental care. "I'm supposed to brush with Sparkle Crest," a six-year-old informed his father after seeing the movie.

What's going on here? This is the "decade of sponsored schools and commercialized classrooms" answers the University of Wisconsin's Center for the Analysis of Commercialism in Education. That's not surprising, considering the budget cuts that have drastically lowered funding for education in most school districts. Schools have enough trouble paying for necessities like books and teachers. They can't begin to afford the extras. So corporations have stepped in.

The Center for the Analysis of Commercialism in Education lists six different ways corporations are finding to get their advertising messages across in schools:

♦ Sponsoring school events like track meets.
♦ Gaining exclusive sales rights to their product—Coke, for instance—on school grounds.
♦ Setting up label-collecting programs.
♦ Providing corporate logo-bearing posters to decorate classrooms.
♦ Offering free educational material such as movies and workbooks.
♦ Donating electronic equipment in return for the right to advertise.

Why the corporate push to advertise to children as young as *five or six*? First, because children have money to spend. In 1997, U.S. children between the ages of four and twelve spent $24.4 billion, three times the amount they spent in 1990.

Children also help spend other people's money. Elementary-school-age children influenced family members, mostly parents, in the spending of $188 billion in 1997—$17.7 billion of it in car sales alone.

It is the third reason for corporate America's interest in children, however, that is the most important. Corporate leaders know that children represent the future. However much money children control or help control today, they will control a great deal more in the years ahead. From a business point of view, children are adult-consumers-in-training.

THE PUSH TO CONSUME

So the advertising blitz doesn't let up at the end of the school day. Like everyone else, young people are inundated with ads. Ads are everywhere, on radio and TV, on streets, and in stores. They're in books, newspapers, and magazines. They're on the Internet. Some ads are glaringly obvious—BUY NOW!!! CALL TODAY!!! Others are so subtle they hardly seem like ads at all.

Watch a movie and note which soft drink an actor picks up or what brand name appears on an actress's jeans. Companies pay good money to "place" their products in this way. Or try counting the ads that appear during the course of a televised sporting event. Not just the few commercials crowded into time-outs or at halftime or between innings, but the never-to-be-ignored advertising billboards that cover all available surfaces in the stadium or arena, the camera shots of banners trailing from blimps and planes overhead, the jocular references to this or that sponsor during the announcers' running commentary.

Notice the ads that appear where none should be. Public "noncommercial" television allows references to Chuck E. Cheese's, McDonald's, and Frosted Flakes during programs like *Arthur* and *Barney & Friends*.[3] Public TV's *Teletubbies* pitches those toys to children too young to walk or talk. "Marketing like this helps encourage that first 'Buy me that' exchange between a parent and a child before the kid even knows how to say 'Buy me that,'" comments Dr. Kathryn Montgomery, president of the Center for Media Education. She and others are appalled by the extent of the commercialism. Merchandisers, by contrast, love it. They see Teletubbies as "filling the one-to-two-year-old niche" in the consumer market.[4]

The local TV news is rife with barely concealed advertising. Stories about crowds turning out for Christmas shopping the day after Thanksgiving aren't really news. The same crowds turn out year after year on that day. Superbowl Sunday stories about football fans stocking up for the big game at sandwich shops, pizza parlors, and delicatessens aren't news either. Yet such stories are given leading spots in the news lineup. They're scripted as if they really were genuine news, making store names and product logos "news" as well. The same companies that advertise their products on a TV station get to see those products promoted during the station's newscasts. Then there are "entertainment news" fillers, thinly veiled promotions for upcoming network specials, movies, and other programming. And what do we see when we tune in to that programming? More ads, more displays of carefully placed products, more references to the vast number of tantalizingly delightful consumer goods and services that no one—*no one*—should have to do without.

That, at bottom, is the message behind the advertising and commercial sponsorship: See it, want it, need it, buy it! The most fashionable clothes, the latest music, the newest video, the trendiest jewelry, the highest-priced sports equipment, the favorite food. Grab them all! Max out on life! Max out on credit! That's what it's for.

USING CREDIT

Is it? Credit is a handy financial tool, no doubt about it. But only if it is used wisely.

How can a person be sure of using credit wisely? It helps to think matters out step by step.

- *Should I get a credit card or take out another type of loan?*

Do you want money to pay for vocational school or college? To buy a car to drive to work? To shop for consumer goods you wouldn't otherwise be able to afford? Do you want a credit card in order to begin establishing a credit history? Think, as you ask yourself such questions, of the ancient Roman distinction between consumptive credit and productive credit. Into which category does an education loan fall? A credit-card bill that comes on the heels of a bout of holiday shopping? What is involved in building a strong credit record? Is it just a matter of owning a credit card?

- *I've decided to get a credit card.*

Which one should you apply for? The one with the highest possible line of credit? One with no annual fee and a moderate APR? A gold card? A card that offers rebates? Any MasterCard because that's the brand you're most familiar with? Visa because your best friend has Visa? An affinity card that identifies you as someone special? Remember that the most important consideration is how much credit ultimately costs. Check a financial guide or Web site for up-to-date information about good credit-card deals.

- *My card has arrived.*

What do you do next? Head for the mall? Celebrate by treating your friends to lunch? Figure out how much you can afford to charge each month? Draw up a budget? Plan on spending up to your credit limit each month?

- *I use my card regularly.*

What do you need to keep in mind? First of all, that despite all the messages from advertisers and commercial sponsors, people do not need to buy everything in sight in order to be happy. Visa has some further suggestions. Make sure your monthly budget includes credit-card payments. To avoid overspending, keep your monthly debt obligation below 10 percent of your monthly after-tax income. Establish a good credit record by using, but not overusing, your card. Never exhaust your credit limit. Pay credit-card bills on time to avoid late fees. Always have enough money on hand to make at least the minimum payment due.[5]

♦ *I'm in trouble!*

You accidentally missed a payment. There seems to be a mistake in your credit file. You are in over your head and can't pay your bills. Don't panic. Help is available. Sometimes a creditor will listen to an explanation and excuse a late payment. That happened to Sally, whom we met in Chapter Five. She called the stores to which she owed money, explained her family emergency, and got several to drop their late-payment charges. If you think there is a mistake in your credit file you have a right to examine it. Call the major credit bureaus and make sure they set the record straight. If you're deeply in debt, try a Consumer Credit Counseling Service.

♦ *I'm determined to repair my poor credit rating.*

In that case, stop charging on your cards at once, says financial writer Andrew Tobias. Cut them up if you think the temptation to use them will be too great. Pay off outstanding bills methodically and, Tobias adds, "vow never even to *open* another of those 30 credit-card solicitations you get in the mail each year."[6]

♦ ♦ ♦

Andrew Tobias has stated that credit cards are great—they are convenient and they make life easier. Quite right. But ease and convenience do not explain why credit cards and the credit industry as a whole exist. The credit industry exists because it is profitable. And as everyone in the business knows, profits flow in most freely when borrowers get into the kind of debt that forces them to pay interest and fees at the highest allowable rates.

By all means take advantage of the credit industry when you really need money for a worthwhile purpose. Just make sure that the industry doesn't end up taking advantage of you.

SOURCE NOTES

CHAPTER ONE

1. Sandy Fertman, "My Biggest Mistake," *The Star-Ledger* (Newark, NJ), December 1–7, 1997, p. 10.
2. Elise Ackerman, "The Debt Junkie," *U.S. News & World Report*, October 20, 1997, p. 74.
3. Gregory La Forge, "Students' high credit-card debts spur states and colleges to act," *The Star-Ledger* (Newark, NJ), November 28, 1997, p. 53.
4. Paul Sweeney, "Until Ed McMahon Calls, They Need to Slice Debt," *The New York Times*, February 22, 1998, Sec. 3, p. 4.
5. Katharine Q. Seelye, "House Approves Legislation to Curb Laws on Bankruptcy," *The New York Times*, June 11, 1988, A22.
6. Sarah McBride, "Young Deadbeats Pose Problems for Credit-Card Issuers," *The Wall Street Journal*, November 11, 1997, B1.
7. "Pace of Consumer Credit Rose in September," *The New York Times*, November 7, 1998, C3.
8. Katharine Q. Seelye, "House to Vote Today on Legislation for Bankruptcy Overhaul," *The New York Times*, June 10, 1988, A18.
9. Andrew Tobias, "Take Control of Your Credit Cards," *Parade*, November 1, 1998, p. 4.
10. Anthony DePalma, "O Canada, Land of Few Banks," *The New York Times*, October 14, 1998, C1.
11. Lewis Mandell, *The Credit Card Industry: A History*, Boston: Twayne Publishers, 1990, p. xviii.

CHAPTER TWO

1. Sura 2: 275.
2. Leviticus 25: 36–7; Ezekiel 18: 8, 13.
3. Sura 2: 279.
4. Jonathan Williams, ed., *Money: A History*, New York: St. Martin's Press, 1997, pp. 18–19.
5. Lewis Mandell, *The Credit Card Industry: A History*, Boston: Twayne Publishers, 1990, p. 12.
6. Jack Weatherford, *The History of Money*, New York: Crown Publishers, Inc., 1997, pp. 20, 22.
7. Williams, pp. 18–19.
8. Weatherford, pp. 27–45.
9. Williams, pp. 34–35.
10. Mandell, p. 13.
11. Weatherford, pp. 41–42.
12. Ibid., p. 48.
13. Williams, pp. 49, 54.
14. Mandell, p. 13.
15. Weatherford, p. 53.
16. Ibid., p. 63; Williams, p. 65.
17. Weatherford, pp. 64–71.
18. Matthew 21: 12–13.
19. Weatherford, p. 68.
20. Barbara W. Tuchman, *A Distant Mirror*, New York: Ballantine Books, 1979, pp. 110–112.
21. Williams, p. 104.
22. Nancy Dunnan, *Banking*, Englewood Cliffs, NJ: Silver Burdett Press, 1990, p. 12.
23. Weatherford, p. 74.
24. Dunnan, p. 39.
25. Joshua Cooper Ramo, "The Big Bank Theory," *Time*, April 27, 1988, p. 47.
26. Weatherford, p. 78.
27. Dunnan, p. 14.
28. Williams, p. 162.
29. Mandell, p. 13.

CHAPTER THREE

1. Lewis Mandell, *The Credit Card Industry: A History*, Boston: Twayne Publishers, 1990, pp. 4, 6.

2. Jenny Uglow, *Hogarth: A Life and a World*, New York: Farrar, Straus and Giroux, 1997, pp. 25–26.
3. Arthur M. Schlesinger, Jr., ed. *The Almanac of American History*, New York: The Putnam Publishing Group, 1983, pp. 82–83.
4. Mandell, p. 15.
5. www.census.gov/population/www/documentation/twps 0027.html
6. Mandell, pp. 14–17.
7. "Poverty Inc.," *Consumer Reports*, July 1998, p. 29.
8. *The World Almanac: 1998*, Mahwah, NJ: K-III Reference Corporation, p. 728.
9. "Credit union," *The World Book Encyclopedia*.
10. Mandell, pp. 14-17.
11. Jack Weatherford, *The History of Money*, New York: Crown Publishers, Inc., 1997, p. 226.
12. Mandell, pp. 1–7.
13. Ibid., pp. 4, 7, 26.
14. Weatherford, p. 227.
15. Mandell, pp. 7, 8, 26.
16. Ibid., pp. 28–32, 34.
17. Ibid, p. 38.
18. Weatherford, p. 227.
19. Mandell, p. xiii.
20. Ibid., p. 35.
21. Ibid., p. xiv.
22. Ibid., p. 48–49.

CHAPTER FOUR

1. Kathy M. Kristof, "Confounding Interest," *The Los Angeles Times*, July 11, 1998, D1.
2. Lewis Mandell, *The Credit Card Industry: A History*, Boston: Twayne Publishers, 1990, p. 72.
3. Stephanie Gallagher, "Fantastic Plastic," *Kiplinger's Personal Finance Magazine*, April 1998, p. 131.
4. John Greenwald, "Charge!," *Time*, January 12, 1988, p. 60.
5. "Credit-card come-ons," *Consumer Reports*, October 1998, p. 56.
6. Margaret Mannix, "Platinum cards can often be fool's gold," *U.S. News & World Report*, January 19, 1998, p. 68.
7. Linda Stern, "Read the Fine Print," *Newsweek*, June 15, 1998, p. 74.

8. Mannix, p. 68.
9. Gallagher, p. 131.
10. Robert D. Hershey, Jr., "That Layered Look in Cash-Advance Fees," *The New York Times*, April 26, 1998, Section 3, p. 9.
11. Stacy Perman, "Good-bye, Freebies—Hello, Fees," *Time*, January 12, 1998, p. 62.
12. Gallagher, p. 131.
13. www.consumer-action.org.
14. Greenwald, p. 60.
15. Mandell, pp. 72–74.
16. Perman, p.62.
17. David Cay Johnston, "Narrowing the Bankruptcy Escape Hatch," *The New York Times*, October 4, 1998, Section 3, p. 9.
18. Timothy L. O'Brien, "Fraud Is Rare, But Check the Tab Anyway," *The New York Times*, November 11, 1998, F1.
19. Perman, p. 62.
20. Kara K. Choquette, "Not all approve of Barbie's MasterCard," *USA Today*, March 30, 1998.
21. "Just who is raking it in?," *Consumer Reports*, September 1998, p. 8.
22. "A question of money," *Consumer Reports*, September 1998, p. 65.
23. "Credit-card come-ons," *Consumer Reports*, October 1998, p. 56.
24. Bob Weinstein, "Campus card games," *The Boston Sunday Globe*, September 6, 1998, N5.
25. "Just who is raking it in?"
26. Gallagher, p. 131.
27. Sumner Lipman, "Crash of the frequent flier," *Capital Weekly* (Augusta, ME), July 9, 1998, A9.
28. Ruth Simon, "Make sure your rebate card still delivers the goods," *Money*, August 1997, p. 42.
29. "Credit-card come-ons."
30. Mannix, p. 68.
31. Sarah McBride, "Young Deadbeats Pose Problems for Credit-Card Issuers," *The Wall Street Journal*, November 28, 1997, B1.
32. Jane Bryant Quinn, "Kids and Credit Cards," *Good Housekeeping*, October 1997, p. 84.
33. Kenneth Z. Chutchian, "Charles talks. Everybody listens," *The Maine Times*, September 3, 1998, p. 4.

34. Al Diamon, "Where the wild things aren't," *Capital Weekly* (Augusta, ME), August 20, 1998, A2.

CHAPTER FIVE

1. Timothy L. O'Brien, "Lowering the Credit Fence," *The New York Times*, December 13, 1997, D1.
2. Bob Weinstein, "Campus card games," *The Boston Sunday Globe*, September 9, 1998, N5.
3. Andrew Tobias, "Take Control of Your Credit Cards," *Parade*, December 1, 1998, p. 4.
4. Gregory La Forge, "Students' high credit-card debts spur states and colleges to act," *The Star-Ledger* (Newark, NJ), November 28, 1997, p. 53.
5. Sharon R. King, "On My...Wall: Thomas Galvin," *The New York Times*, September 27, 1998, Section 3, p. 2.
6. Ellen Stark, "How to stop a debit card from draining your account," *Money*, November 1997, p. 45.
7. Joel Brinkley, "Judge Orders a Credit Bureau to Stop Selling Consumer Lists," *The New York Times*, August 27, 1998, A14.
8. Lewis Mandell, *The Credit Card Industry: A History*, Boston: Twayne Publishers, 1990, pp. 59–60.
9. Brinkley, A14.
10. Brett Pulley, "Those Seductive Snake Eyes: Tales of Growing Up Gambling," *The New York Times*, June 16, 1998, A1.
11. Katharine Q. Seelye, "House Approves Legislation To Curb Laws on Bankruptcy," *The New York Times*, June 11, 1988, A22.
12. Kerry Hannon, "Wiping the Slate Clean," *U.S. News & World Report*, October 20, 1997, p. 84.
13. Jean Sherman Chatzky, "Hidden dangers: How insurers set your rates," *Money*, April 1998, p. 204.
14. "Poverty Inc.," *Consumer Reports*, July 1998, p. 29.
15. "Bare-knuckles banking," *Consumer Reports*, December 1998, p. 8.
16. "Poverty Inc."
17. O'Brien, D1.
18. Joshua Cooper Ramo, "The Big Bank Theory," *Time*, April 27, 1988, p. 47.
19. Peter T. Kilborn, "New Lenders With Huge Fees Thrive on Workers With Debts," *The New York Times*, June 18, 1999, A1.
20. "Poverty Inc."

21. "Queens Grocer Charged In Death of Couple," *The New York Times*, May 20, 1998, B6.

CHAPTER SIX

1. Gregory La Forge, "Students' high credit-card debts spur states and colleges to act," *The Star-Ledger* (Newark, NJ), November 28, 1997, p. 53.
2. Bob Weinstein, "Campus card games," *The Boston Sunday Globe*, September 9, 1998, N5.
3. Lewis Mandell, *The Credit Card Industry: A History*, Boston: Twayne Publishers, 1990, pp. 33–37, 52–60.
4. "New ways to fix your credit file," *Money*, October 1997, p. 44.
5. "Poverty Inc.," *Consumer Reports*, July 1998, p. 29.
6. Timothy L. O'Brien, "Lowering the Credit Fence," *The New York Times*, December 13, 1997, D1.
7. Robert D. Hershey, Jr., "The Sky Is Becoming the Only Limit for Credit Card Users," *The New York Times*, August 9, 1998, Section 3, p. 11.
8. "Stats," *Yahoo Internet Life*, January 1999, p. 86.
9. "New Internet Loan Services Are Not for the Faint of Heart," *The New York Times*, July 2, 1998, G3.
10. "Protecting your privacy," *Consumer Reports*, November 1998, p. 23.
11. Rob Fixmer, "Tiny New Chip Could Pit Protection of Property Against Right of Privacy," *The New York Times*, September 29, 1998, F6.
12. Carol Marie Cropper, "Teaching the Teachers About Investing," *The New York Times*, April 12, 1998, Sec. 3, p. 10.
13. Fixmer, F6.
14. Saul Hansell, "Got a Dime? Citibank and Chase End Test of Electronic Cash," *The New York Times*, November 4, 1998, C1.
15. "Credit counseling," *Consumer Reports*, September 1998, p. 65.
16. Anthony Ramirez, "Chase Bank Finds Room for Small Borrowers," *The New York Times*, December 10, 1998, B26.
17. "Poverty Inc."
18. Richard A. Oppel Jr., "The Stepchildren of Banking," *The New York Times*, March 3, 1999, C1.
19. Sarah McBride, "Young Deadbeats Pose Problems for Credit-Card Issuers," *The Wall Street Journal*, November 11, 1997, B1.

CHAPTER SEVEN

1. Kara K. Choquette, "Not all approve of Barbie's MasterCard," *USA Today*, March 30, 1998.

2. Constance L. Hays, "First Lessons in the Power of Money," *The New York Times*, April 12, 1998, Sec. 3, p. 1.

3. "Reading, writing, and...buying?," *Consumer Reports*, September 1998, p. 45.

4. Lawrie Mifflin, "Critics Assail PBS Over Plan For Toys Aimed at Toddlers," *The New York Times*, April 20, 1998, A1.

5. "Five tips for college students using credit cards," *The Boston Sunday Globe*, September 6, 1998, N7.

6. Andrew Tobias, "Take Control of Your Credit Cards," *Parade*, December 1, 1998, p. 4.

FOR FURTHER INFORMATION

Books

Detweiler, Gerri. *The Ultimate Credit Handbook.* New York: Penguin Books USA, 1993.

Mandell, Lewis. *The Credit Card Industry: A History.* Boston: Twayne Publishers, 1990.

Weatherford, Jack. *The History of Money.* New York: Crown Publishers, Inc., 1997.

Williams, Jonathan, ed. *Money: A History.* New York: St. Martin's Press, 1997.

Brochures

"Plastic Made Simple"
MasterCard International
Attn: Fulfillment Center
1970 Craigshire
St. Louis, MO 63146

"Managing Your Debt"
Consumer Federation of America
P.O. Box 12099
Washington, D.C. 20005-0999
(include self-addressed, stamped, business-size envelope)

CREDIT BUREAU TELEPHONE NUMBERS

Equifax: 888-909-7304

Experian: 800-353-0809

Trans Union: 888-5-OPT-OUT   or   888-567-8688

CREDIT COUNSELING

National Foundation for Consumer Credit: 800-388-2227 for a member credit counseling agency

INTERNET RESOURCES

Bank Rate Monitor: **www.bankrate.com**

CardWeb Inc.: **www.cardtrak.com**

Consumer Action: **www.consumer-action.org**

Consumer Reports: **www.ConsumerReports.org**

National Institute for Consumer Education, Eastern Michigan University: **www.emich.edu/public/coe/nice**

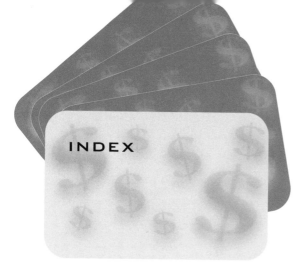

INDEX